Splash!

Modeling and Measurement Applications for Young Learners

a mathematics unit for high-ability learners in grades k–1

Splash!

Modeling and Measurement Applications for Young Learners

Virginia Caine Tonneson, Ph.D.

The College of William and Mary
School of Education
Center for Gifted Education
P.O. Box 8795
Williamsburg, VA 23187

Center for Gifted Education Staff:
Executive Director: Dr. Tracy L. Cross
Curriculum Director: Dr. Kimberley L. Chandler
Curriculum Writer: Dr. Virginia Caine Tonneson
Content Advisor: Dr. Janice I. Robbins

Center for Gifted Education
The College of William & Mary

Routledge
Taylor & Francis Group
NEW YORK AND LONDON

First published in 2013 by Prufrock Press Inc.

Published in 2021 by Routledge
605 Third Avenue, New York, NY 10017
2 Park Square, Milton Park, Abingdon, Oxon OX14 4RN

Routledge is an imprint of the Taylor & Francis Group, an informa business

Production design by Raquel Trevino

ISBN: 9781593639709 (pbk)

DOI: 10.4324/9781003238171

Contents

Part One: Introduction

Introduction to the Unit 1

Unit Materials 13

Assessment 14

Unit Glossary 14

Part Two: Lesson Plans

Lesson 1: Preassessment 18

Lesson 2: Models 23

Lesson 3: Dimensions 29

Lesson 4: Comparing and Ordering Objects 40

Lesson 5: Partitioning 44

Lesson 6: Comparing Length by Rearranging Parts (Decomposing and Recomposing) 47

Lesson 7: Linear Measurement: Measuring Length Using Nonstandard Units 54

Lesson 8: Linear Measurement: Measuring Distance Using Nonstandard Units 57

Lesson 9: Linear Measurement: Measuring Height Using Nonstandard Units 63

Lesson 10: Linear Measurement: Measuring Length Using Standard Units 66

Lesson 11: Linear Measurement: Appropriate Units and Tools 70

Lesson 12: Measuring Perimeter 73

Lesson 13: Postassessment 79

Part Three: Unit Extension and References

Unit Extension: Building a Pool 86

References 89

Common Core State Standards Alignment 91

Part One: Introduction

Introduction to the Unit

Unit Overview: *Splash! Modeling and Measurement Applications for Young Learners* is a unit for students in kindergarten and first grade that focuses on the mathematical concepts related to linear measurement, the creativity elements of fluency and flexibility, and the overarching, interdisciplinary concept of models. The unit consists of 13 lessons centered on the idea of designing a community pool. Students examine the question of why we measure, the importance of accuracy in measurement, and the various units and tools of measurement. The unit presents a hands-on, constructivist approach, allowing children to build their knowledge base and their skills as they explore mathematical ideas through play and planned investigations. Students are involved in creative and critical thinking, problem solving, process skill development, and communication opportunities.

Essential Understandings in Mathematics:

- Objects with different attributes are measured in different ways (appropriate measurement).
- An item remains the same length even when placed in a different position (conservation).
- Knowing the relationship between one item and a second item, and between the second item and a third item, one may deduce the relationship between the first item and third item (transitivity).
- The length of an object can be divided into equal-sized units (partitioning).
- Accurate measurements require identical units, precise starting and ending points, no gaps or overlaps in coverage, and partitioning of leftover (non-whole) units (measurement accuracy).
- The length of a larger unit may be made up of repeating smaller units (unit iteration).
- Certain units convey what is being measured better than others (appropriate units).
- Certain tools work better than others to measure the same attributes (appropriate tools).
- The larger the unit of measure, the smaller the number of units needed to measure a particular object; the smaller the unit of measure, the larger the number of units needed to measure that same object (inverse relationship between size of units and number of units).

Unit Concept Map: This concept map (see Figure 1) illustrates various measurement ideas presented in this unit and their relationships to each other. Some concepts, such as area and volume, are not directly taught in this unit, but can easily be discussed as extensions.

Overarching Concept: The overarching, interdisciplinary concept for this unit is *models*. Students come to understand that models are simplifications of objects, ideas, or processes. Models can be physical, conceptual, or mathematical. In this unit, students learn more about the usefulness of physical models.

The second lesson in this unit introduces the concept of models. Students generate a list of examples of models and then categorize their examples, identify nonexamples, and make generalizations about models. The following generalizations are supported by and incorporated into the unit lessons.

DOI: 10.4324/9781003238171-2

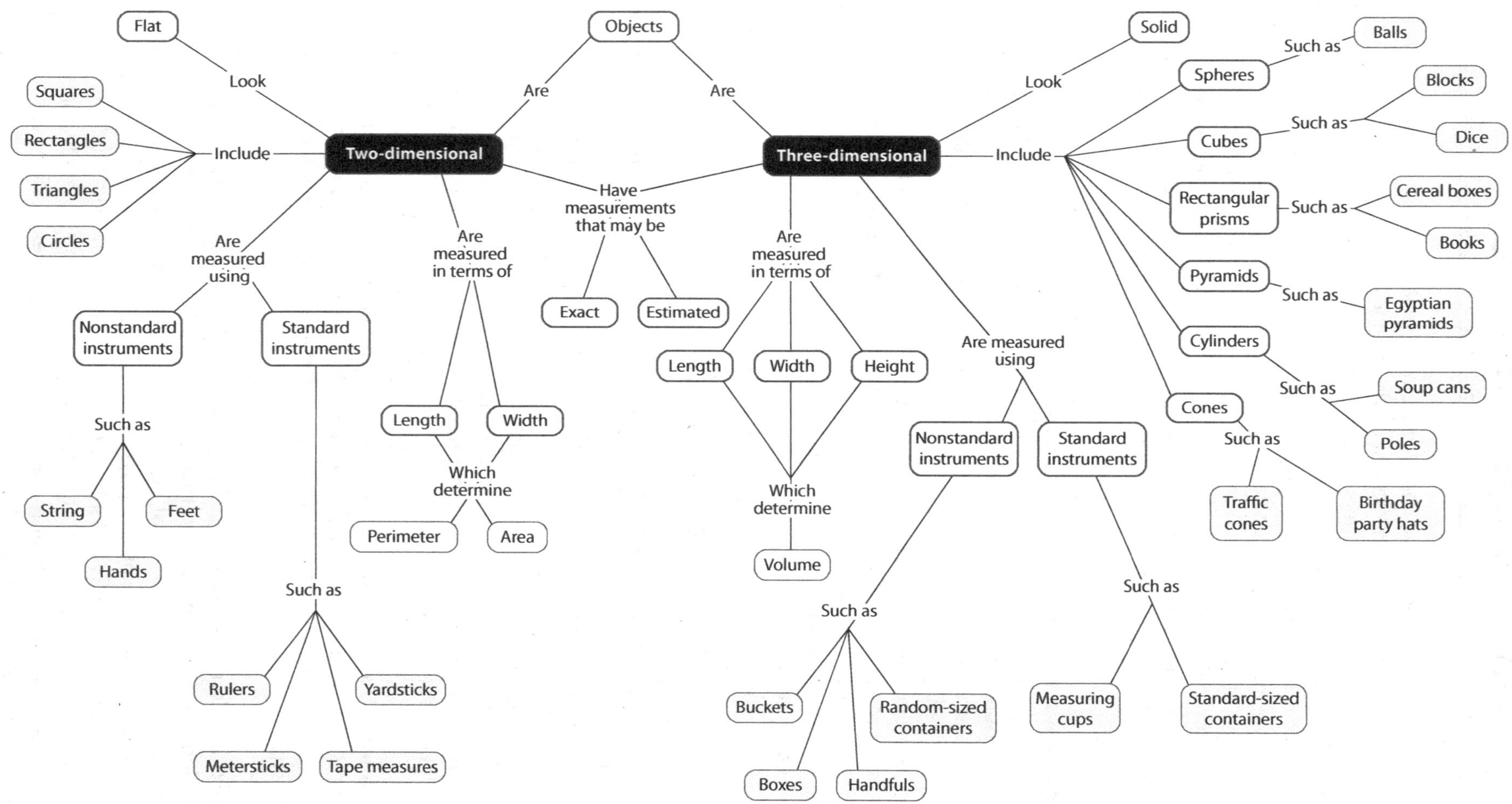

Figure 1. Unit concept map.

- Real things can be represented by pictures, drawings, diagrams, objects, or actions.
- Models are simpler and often smaller versions of something.
- People use models to help solve problems.
- Models can be used to test ideas, solutions, and plans.
- Mathematicians use mathematical models to provide ways to solve problems using numbers.

Main Ideas in Mathematics: This unit builds on nine main ideas.

- *Objects with different attributes are measured in different ways (appropriate measurement).* Therefore, one might talk about the depth of a swimming pool, but not the depth of a sign painted on a wall. Similarly, one measures the length, width, and height of a three-dimensional object, but only the length and width of a two-dimensional object.
- *An item remains the same length even when placed in a different position (conservation).* Therefore, a 2-foot-long stick will remain that length whether it is lying flat, standing on its end, or leaning at an angle. Similarly, two items of equal length will remain equal even when they are moved to different positions in relation to each other.
- *Knowing the relationship between one item and a second item, and between the second item and a third item, one may deduce the relationship between the first item and third item (transitivity).* Therefore, if a child and a stick are the same height, and the stick and a bookcase are the same height, then the child and the bookcase will be the same height. An understanding of transitivity is necessary for students to make indirect comparisons.
- *The length of an object can be divided into equal-sized units (partitioning).* Therefore, a piece of string can be folded into four equal lengths.
- *Accurate measurements require identical units, precise starting and ending points, no gaps or overlaps in coverage, and partitioning of leftover (non-whole) units (measurement accuracy).* Therefore, if one wants to measure the height of the middle shelf of a bookshelf, the starting point is no longer at the bottom of the bookshelf, nor is the ending point at the top of the bookshelf. One would measure the bookshelf using like units, such as inches, and would express the non-whole remaining units as some portion of an inch.
- *The length of a larger unit may be made up of repeating smaller units (unit iteration).* Therefore, a table may be measured by repeatedly placing a craft stick along its length and counting how many craft sticks long the table is. A child who has not yet developed the logic of unit iteration may tell you that the craft stick is too short to measure the table.
- *Certain units convey what is being measured better than others (appropriate units).* Therefore, one might use inches to measure the length of a piece of string, but not to measure the length of a swimming pool.
- *Certain tools work better than others to measure the same attributes (appropriate tools).* Therefore, one might use a ruler to measure a short piece of string, but a tape measure to measure the length of a room.
- *The larger the unit of measure, the smaller the number of units needed to measure a particular object; the smaller the unit of measure, the larger the number of units needed to measure that same object (inverse relationship between size of units and number of units).* Therefore, an object that measures 10 craft sticks long may measure 36 paper clips long.

Supporting Ideas in Mathematics: There are several other important supporting mathematical concepts that this unit touches upon:

- *Items may be grouped by comparing and contrasting their attributes (classification).* Therefore, while two objects may each have a length and a width, if one also has a height, it becomes part of a different group (three-dimensional objects).
- *Sometimes a close approximation of a number is accurate enough (rounding).* Therefore, saying the length of a table is "about 20 craft sticks long" may be a less precise but more manageable measurement.
- *Sets of items may look different, but represent the same amount (equivalence).* Therefore, 29 paper clips laid end-to-end, 8 craft sticks laid end-to-end, and a yardstick could represent the same length.
- *Using what you know about two objects may be helpful in estimating an attribute of one of the objects.* Therefore, one might reason that because the smaller table is 20 craft sticks long, the larger table is approximately 30 craft sticks long.

Critical Thinking Skills:

- Students should be taught to think about their mathematical reasoning (metacognition) and should be encouraged to explain the strategies they used to get their answers. How do they know their answer is correct?
- Students need to understand the connections between mathematics and the world around them. They should develop an understanding of how mathematics is an integral part of science, business, social sciences, medicine, and engineering, as well as how mathematics impacts their everyday life.
- Students should be encouraged to think about mathematical problems in different ways. By learning problem-solving strategies early on, students will find it much easier to build on what they know about a problem so they can reason out what they don't know. Thus, building fluency and flexibility into ideation is essential.
- Students should be taught critical thinking skills. They should learn how to describe problematic situations or issues and compare similarities and differences. It is also important for them to learn how to describe evidence, support conclusions, predict consequences, and define relevant concepts.
- Students should understand the different ways that modeling is used within mathematics. The process of problem solving can be modeled. Physical models can be used as manipulatives to aid understanding of mathematical concepts or to represent actual items.

Problem Solving: Each lesson begins with a *Thinking About the Problem* section to encourage the students to think carefully about the process of solving a problem. Read the short scenario and allow the students to talk about the problem. Create a "Need to Know" board to use as a metacognitive planner and complete it with the students' responses to the following questions:

- What do we know?
- What do we need to know?
- How can we find out?

Revisit the board at the end of each lesson to see if students were able to solve the problem.

Gifted Student Preferences: Teachers of gifted students must recognize the different ways in which children process information. Many typical students are field-*indepen-*

dent learners, which means they use *successive* thought processing to understand a new concept. In essence, they look at the pieces first and then build upon those bits of knowledge to see the whole picture (Hatfield, Edwards, Bitter, & Morrow, 2000). In contrast, many gifted students are field-*dependent* learners, using *simultaneous* thought processing to see the whole first, and subsequently to break it into its respective parts by looking for relationships and patterns. Because of this, gifted students are more likely to learn effectively when a concept is taught whole-to-part, rather than part-to-whole (Rogers, 2008). In other words, when describing a ruler, a teacher could put 12 individual inches together to show the measurement of a foot (part-to-whole) or could instead introduce the entire ruler as "a foot" and then break it into 12 inches (whole-to-part).

Length of Lessons: Each lesson is designed to take approximately 45 minutes; however, the lessons may easily be modified by adding or subtracting activities. Additionally, most of the lessons provide extension activities to enhance student learning. The pre- and postassessment lessons can be easily adjusted to cover the material selected to be covered in the unit.

Timing: This unit can typically be completed in 2–3 weeks in a classroom setting; however, the overarching concept of models can be eliminated if classroom time is limited. In addition, the *Building a Pool* extension activity is time consuming because it requires the teacher to help students individually to physically put the swimming pool together. If a teacher decides to complete this activity, it is highly recommended that he or she solicit parent volunteers to assist. Table 1 shows the suggested timeframe for the lessons depending on the students' skill level.

Extension Activities: In addition to the lesson-specific extension activities, several lessons also include *Building a Pool* extension activities to enhance the students' learning experience. (The materials needed to support the *Building a Pool* extension are identified with a wave-shaped symbol.) These extension activities build upon one another, guiding students to create an actual three-dimensional model of a swimming pool from a plastic container and foam core board. A teacher may decide to do these *Building a Pool* extension activities along with particular lessons, or may instead decide to do the entire extension project at the conclusion of the unit. An explanation about how to build the pool is included in Part Three: Unit Extension and References.

Background Information: Measurement is used all around us. We use it to talk about time, to measure distances, and to cook. Forming a strong basis of measurement concepts is essential for young students, as it supports not only other mathematical ideas, such as numbers and geometry, but also everyday skills. The National Council of Teachers of Mathematics (NCTM, 2000) has stated that linear measurement should be the primary focus for young elementary students in developing conceptual measurement foundations.

Battista (2006) pointed out that the concept of length is more complex than it initially seems. He explained that although the dictionary definition of "length" refers to the straight-line distance from endpoint to endpoint, mathematically, length would be measured along the entire distance. The discrepancy becomes apparent when one visualizes a crooked road. Do we measure the length "as the crow flies," or do we measure the distance traveled? He further pointed out that length may have confusing connotations for children when related to time (How *long* until dinner?), distance (How *long* is this road?), and spatial magnitude (Which dimensions are the *length*, width, and height of this box?). He broke student reasoning about length into eight different stages. The

Table 1

Suggested Lessons for Various Classroom Needs

Minimum Treatment of the Unit	Intermediate Treatment of the Unit	Maximum Treatment of the Unit
• For younger students and students requiring more support • For classrooms where limited time is available	• For students who are unfamiliar with the material • For classrooms where there is time to complete fewer than 11 lessons	• For students who are very capable • For classrooms where there is time to complete at least 11 lessons
• Cover Lessons 3–7, 10 • Select only specific activities within the lessons	• Cover Lessons 3–8, 10–12 • Select only a few extensions • Show the class a premade pool from the Building a Pool extension activity and allow students to measure various attributes	• Cover all lessons and many lesson-specific extensions • Have individual students create a pool using the Building a Pool extension activity
• Reduce the time devoted to pre- and postassessment (in Lessons 1 and 13) by eliminating the math process and overarching concept sections	• Reduce the time devoted to pre- and postassessments (in Lessons 1 and 13) by eliminating the overarching concept section	• Use all pre- and postassessment components (in Lessons 1 and 13)

first three require "nonmeasurement" reasoning (numbers are not used), whereas the following five stages use measurement reasoning (numbers are used):

1. *Holistic Visual Comparison:* Students look at whole shapes and compare them using either direct or indirect comparison.
2. *Comparison by Decomposing or Recomposing:* Students rearrange parts for direct comparison or match pieces one-to-one.
3. *Comparison by Property-Based Transformations:* Students compare lengths by turning, sliding, or flipping shapes so that the transformed shapes are congruent.
4. *Use of Numbers Unconnected to Unit Iteration:* Students count to determine lengths, but the counting does not represent a uniform unit length.
5. *Incorrect Unit Iteration:* Students attempt unit iteration but leave gaps and overlaps and may use various lengths as their unit.
6. *Correct Unit Iteration:* Students correctly use unit iteration without leaving gaps or overlaps or variation in unit length.
7. *Operating on Iterations:* Students use unit iteration to make logical inferences or to conduct numerical operations on iterated or inferred measurements.
8. *Operating on Numerical Measurements:* Students operate numerically or inferentially without initially using unit iteration.

Curriculum Framework: The Curriculum Framework (see Table 2) lists the core goals and related student outcomes that frame the book's lessons.

Links to Common Core State Standards and NCTM Standards: This unit addresses the Common Core State Standards for Mathematics for kindergarten, grade 1, and grade 2, with the expectation that some advanced students in K–1 will be working at a second-grade level:

Table 2

Curriculum Framework

Goal	Student Outcomes ***The student will be able to:***
1. Develop an understanding of the concept of models as they relate to the mathematical content goals.	• Provide examples and nonexamples of models. • Categorize lists of models. • Express generalizations about models.
2. Develop knowledge of specific mathematical concepts related to measurement.	• Use appropriate measurement words to describe objects. • Compare and give examples of two- and three-dimensional objects. • Compare and order objects using appropriate terminology (greater than, less than, equal to). • Partition objects into equal parts and recognize that equal parts can be put together to create a whole. • Identify a measurement's starting and ending points. • Demonstrate measuring with no gaps or overlaps using standard and nonstandard tools. • Specify "leftover" units by using both rounding words and mathematical terminology. • Explain why standard units are needed and why units need to be identical within a measurement. • Demonstrate equivalent ways of measuring. • Estimate the length of an object given another object of similar length. • Select appropriate units and tools to measure various items. • Explain the purpose of finding a perimeter of an object. • Find the perimeter of regularly shaped objects. • Estimate the perimeter of an object given one of similar size.
3. Develop critical thinking skills.	• Define relevant concepts. • Describe similarities and differences. • Describe evidence and support conclusions. • Predict consequences.
4. Develop creative thinking skills.	• Develop fluency in generating ideas. • Develop flexibility in articulating ideas. • Demonstrate originality and elaboration.
5. Develop problem-solving strategies.	• Summarize problem situations, explaining what is known and what is needed. • Collaborate to gather data and find solutions. • Develop a solution/resolution to the problem.
6. Develop interest and curiosity in the world of mathematics.	• Ask meaningful questions about mathematical topics. • Articulate ideas of interest about mathematics. • Demonstrate persistence in completing mathematical tasks.

- Kindergarten: Describe and compare measurable attributes (Common Core State Standards Initiative, 2010, p. 12).
- Kindergarten: Classify objects and count the number of objects in each category (Common Core State Standards Initiative, 2010, p. 12).
- Grade 1: Measure lengths indirectly and by iterating length units (Common Core State Standards Initiative, 2010, p. 16).
- Grade 2: Measure and estimate lengths in standard units (Common Core State Standards Initiative, 2010, p. 20).

This unit addresses the NCTM Measurement Standards for Pre-K–2:

- Understand measurable attributes of objects and the units, systems, and processes of measurement; and
- Apply appropriate techniques, tools, and formulas to determine measurement (NCTM, 2000, p. 102).

NCTM also identifies Essential Expectations for Measurement for Pre-K–2:

Students should be able to:

- recognize the attributes of length, volume, weight, area, and time;
- compare and order objects according to these attributes;
- understand how to measure using nonstandard and standard units;
- select an appropriate unit and tool for the attribute being measured;
- measure with multiple copies of units of the same size, such as paper clips laid end to end;
- use repetition of a single unit to measure something larger than the unit, for instance, measuring the length of a room with a single meterstick;
- use tools to measure;
- develop common referents for measures to make comparisons and estimates. (NCTM, 2000, p. 102)

Table 3 shows which lessons address each particular NCTM expectation.

Lesson Plan Blueprint: The Lesson Plan Blueprint (see Table 4) breaks down each lesson, providing the instructional purpose, overarching concept, essential mathematical understandings, and creative and critical thinking skills and problem-solving skills covered in the lesson.

Table 3

NCTM Expectations Addressed by Lessons

NCTM Expectation	Lesson
Recognize the attributes of length, volume, weight, area, and time	3: Dimensions 5: Partitioning
Compare and order objects according to these attributes	3: Dimensions 4: Comparing and Ordering Objects 6: Comparing Length by Rearranging Parts (Decomposing and Recomposing)
Understand how to measure using nonstandard and standard units	7: Linear Measurement: Measuring Length Using Nonstandard Units 8: Linear Measurement: Measuring Distance Using Nonstandard Units 9: Linear Measurement: Measuring Height Using Nonstandard Units 10: Linear Measurement: Measuring Length Using Standard Units 11: Linear Measurement: Appropriate Units and Tools 12: Measuring Perimeter
Select an appropriate unit and tool for the attribute being measured	11: Linear Measurement: Appropriate Units and Tools 12: Measuring Perimeter
Measure with multiple copies of units of the same size, such as paper clips laid end to end	7: Linear Measurement: Measuring Length Using Nonstandard Units 8: Linear Measurement: Measuring Distance Using Nonstandard Units 9: Linear Measurement: Measuring Height Using Nonstandard Units 10: Linear Measurement: Measuring Length Using Standard Units 11: Linear Measurement: Appropriate Units and Tools 12: Measuring Perimeter
Use repetition of a single unit to measure something larger than the unit, for instance, measuring the length of a room with a single meterstick	7: Linear Measurement: Measuring Length Using Nonstandard Units 8: Linear Measurement: Measuring Distance Using Nonstandard Units 9: Linear Measurement: Measuring Height Using Nonstandard Units 10: Linear Measurement: Measuring Length Using Standard Units 11: Linear Measurement: Appropriate Units and Tools 12: Measuring Perimeter
Use tools to measure	10: Linear Measurement: Measuring Length Using Standard Units 11: Linear Measurement: Appropriate Units and Tools 12: Measuring Perimeter
Develop common referents for measures to make comparisons and estimates	7: Linear Measurement: Measuring Length Using Nonstandard Units 8: Linear Measurement: Measuring Distance Using Nonstandard Units 9: Linear Measurement: Measuring Height Using Nonstandard Units 10: Linear Measurement: Measuring Length Using Standard Units 11: Linear Measurement: Appropriate Units and Tools 12: Measuring Perimeter

Table 4

Lesson Plan Blueprint

Lesson #	Title	Instructional Purpose	Overarching Concept (Models)	Essential Mathematical Understandings	Creative and Critical Thinking Skills/Problem Solving
1	Preassessment	• To assess student knowledge and understanding of unit topics			
2	Models	• To introduce the idea of models	• Real things and processes can be represented by pictures, drawings, diagrams, objects, or actions. • Models are simpler and often smaller versions of something. • People use models to help them solve problems. • Models can be used to test out ideas.	• A model is a physical, conceptual, or mathematical simplification of an object or process.	• Fluency • Flexibility • Elaboration • Originality • Problem finding • Searching for information • Communicating ideas
3	Dimensions	• To introduce the idea of dimensions	• Real things and processes can be represented by pictures, drawings, diagrams, objects, or actions. • Models are simpler and often smaller versions of something.	• Objects with different attributes are measured in different ways (appropriate measurement). • Items may be grouped by comparing and contrasting their attributes (classification).	• Fluency • Elaboration • Originality • Problem finding • Searching for information • Communicating ideas
4	Comparing and Ordering Objects	• To compare and order objects by length	• Real things and processes can be represented by pictures, drawings, diagrams, objects, or actions. • People use models to help them solve problems.	• An item remains the same length even when placed in a different position (conservation). • Knowing the relationship between one item and a second item, and the second item and a third item, one may deduce the relationship between the first item and third item (transitivity).	• Fluency • Flexibility • Originality • Problem finding • Searching for information • Communicating ideas • Drawing conclusions
5	Partitioning	• To visualize how whole objects can be partitioned	• Models are simpler and often smaller versions of something.	• The length of an object can be divided into equal-sized units (partitioning). • Sets of items may look different, but represent the same amount (equivalence).	• Flexibility • Problem finding • Searching for information • Communicating ideas • Drawing conclusions

Table 4, *continued*

Lesson #	Title	Instructional Purpose	Overarching Concept (Models)	Essential Mathematical Understandings	Creative and Critical Thinking Skills/Problem Solving
6	Comparing Length by Rearranging Parts (Decomposing and Recomposing)	• To compare length by repeating smaller units	• Real things and processes can be represented by pictures, drawings, diagrams, and objects.	• The length of an object can be divided into equal-sized units (partitioning). • The length of a larger unit may be made up of repeating smaller units (unit iteration).	• Elaboration • Originality • Problem finding • Searching for information • Communicating ideas • Drawing conclusions
7	Linear Measurement: Measuring Length Using Nonstandard Units	• To explore the fundamentals of accurate measurement	• Real things and processes can be represented by pictures, drawings, diagrams, objects, or actions. • People use models to help them solve problems.	• Accurate measurements require identical units, precise starting and ending points, no gaps or overlaps in coverage, and partitioning of leftover (non-whole) units (measurement accuracy). • The length of an object can be divided into equal-sized units (partitioning). • The length of a larger unit may be made up of repeating smaller units (unit iterations). • The larger the unit of measure, the smaller the number of units needed to measure a particular object; the smaller the unit, the larger the number of units needed to measure that same object (inverse relationship between size of units and number of units). • Sometimes a close approximation of a number is accurate enough (rounding). • Sets of items may look different, but represent the same amount (equivalence).	• Fluency • Problem finding • Searching for information • Communicating ideas • Drawing conclusions
8	Linear Measurement: Measuring Distance Using Nonstandard Units	• To measure distance accurately using nonstandard units	• Real things and processes can be represented by pictures, drawings, diagrams, objects, or actions.	• Accurate measurements require identical units, precise starting and ending points, no gaps or overlaps in coverage, and partitioning of leftover (non-whole) units (measurement accuracy). • The length of a larger unit may be made up of repeating smaller units (unit iteration). • Sets of items may look different, but represent the same amount (equivalence).	• Originality • Problem finding • Searching for information • Communicating ideas • Drawing conclusions
9	Linear Measurement: Measuring Height Using Nonstandard Units	• To measure height accurately using nonstandard units	• Models are simpler and often smaller versions of something.	• The length of an object can be divided into equal-sized units (partitioning). • The length of a larger unit may be made up of repeating smaller units (unit iteration). • Knowing the relationship between one item and a second item, and the second item and a third item, one may deduce the relationship between the first item and third item (transitivity). • Certain units convey what is being measured better than others (appropriate units).	• Fluency • Flexibility • Problem finding • Searching for information • Communicating ideas • Drawing conclusions

Table 4, *continued*

Lesson #	Title	Instructional Purpose	Overarching Concept (Models)	Essential Mathematical Understandings	Creative and Critical Thinking Skills/Problem Solving
10	Linear Measurement: Measuring Length Using Standard Units	• To introduce standard units • To measure accurately using standard measurement tools	• Real things and processes can be represented by pictures, drawings, diagrams, objects, or actions. • Models are simpler and often smaller versions of something.	• Accurate measurements require identical units, precise starting and ending points, no gaps or overlaps in coverage, and partitioning of leftover (non-whole) units (measurement accuracy). • Using what you know about an object may be helpful in making an educated guess about the numerical approximation of an object (estimation).	• Originality • Problem finding • Searching for information • Communicating ideas
11	Linear Measurement: Appropriate Units and Tools	• To familiarize students with various measurement tools and their uses	• Real things and processes can be represented by pictures, drawings, diagrams, objects, or actions.	• The larger the unit of measure, the smaller the number of units needed to measure a particular object; the smaller the unit, the larger the number of units needed to measure that same object (inverse relationship between size of units and number of units). • Certain units convey what is being measured better than others (appropriate units). • Certain tools work better than others to measure the same attributes (appropriate tools).	• Problem finding • Searching for information • Communicating ideas • Drawing conclusions
12	Measuring Perimeter	• To introduce the concept of perimeter	• Real things and processes can be represented by pictures, drawings, diagrams, objects, or actions. • Models can be used to test out things.	• Objects with different attributes are measured in different ways (appropriate measurement). • An item remains the same length even when placed in a different position (conservation). • Certain units convey what is being measured better than others (appropriate units). • Certain tools work better than others to measure different attributes (appropriate tools). • Using what you know about an object may be helpful in making an educated guess about the numerical approximation of an object (estimation).	• Fluency • Flexibility • Originality • Elaboration • Problem finding • Searching for information • Communicating ideas • Drawing conclusions
13	Postassessment	• To assess student knowledge and understanding of unit topics		• Objects with different attributes are measured in different ways (appropriate measurement).	

Unit Materials

- Adding machine paper roll
- Aquarium (or other large container to fill with water)
- Bag (to hold various 2-D and 3-D items)
- Ball
- Blocks of various sizes
- Blue bond paper
- Blue painter's tape or masking tape
- Books of various sizes
- Bookshelf (or other item to demonstrate inward depth measurement)
- Boxes (8" and 12" tall)
- Cardstock
- Construction paper (several colors)
- Containers (e.g., cup, trashcan, plastic containers)
- Counters
- Craft sticks
- Crayons or markers
- Dice or other rectangular prisms
- *Dinosaurs Before Dark* (Magic Tree House series) by Mary Pope Osborne and Sal Murdocca (Random House) or any other book with a picture of a tree house
- Dowels (6" and 12" tall)
- Drawing or picture of above-ground and below-ground swimming pools
- Geoboards (plastic boards with small knobs over which to stretch rubber bands)
- Glue
- House blueprint
- Index cards
- Legos®
- "Lifeguard Lucy" (a doll about 2" tall)
- Masking or clear tape
- *Math Counts: Length* by Henry Pluckrose (Children's Press)
- Meterstick
- *Millions to Measure* by David M. Schwartz (HarperCollins)
- Miscellaneous classroom objects of various sizes (for pre- and postassessment)
- Model car and corresponding photo of actual car
- Model of molecule
- Paper clips
- Paper party nut containers (small paper cups such as those used for ketchup at fast-food restaurants)
- Paper roll (large size to make person's outline)
- Pencils
- Pipe cleaners
- Plastic straws
- Plate
- Play-Doh™ or clay
- Ribbons (approximately 1" wide, various colors)
- Rulers (with inches and centimeters)
- Scissors
- Sponge animal (the type that expands when water is added)
- Stapler

DOI: 10.4324/9781003238171-3

- Sticky notes
- Strips of paper (adding machine paper works well)
- Tape measures (hardware type and sewing type)
- Toothpicks (flat)
- Trundle wheel
- Unifix™ cubes (or other stacking cubes of multiple colors)
- Water
- Yardstick
- Yarn

Assessment

Regular formative assessment is crucial to effective instruction. In order for teachers to know where to focus their instruction, they need to have a good understanding of what their students currently understand. By continually assessing students *for* learning as they proceed with the lesson, teachers are able to immediately build on this knowledge to modify their feedback, their instruction, and the activities in which their students are engaged. This ongoing assessment informs the teacher about what is and is not working in the lesson, which allows a focus on the strategies that will best meet the objectives. This ongoing assessment is in contrast to assessment *of* learning, where the teacher is assessing what a child has learned after the fact. In combination, both types of assessment can provide the teacher with tools to monitor student progress effectively. At the conclusion of each lesson, there is a suggested assessment, but teachers may select different methods to measure the students' levels of understanding.

- **Preassessment:** The preassessment is aimed at determining student knowledge and understanding of unit topics. It focuses on three major areas: math content (representation, measurement, estimation, comparison), math processes (problem solving), and the overarching concept (models).
- **Postassessment:** The postassessment parallels the structure of the preassessment. Teachers who administer both assessments should be able to determine whether students understand the concepts presented in this unit.

Unit Glossary

Approximate: To estimate a number, often by rounding to the nearest whole number or to the nearest 10.

Centimeter: A metric unit of length equal to approximately 0.3937 inches.

Depth: A dimension measured downward or inward.

End point: The point at which a measurement stops.

Equal to (=): Being the same (e.g., 3 – 1 = 4).

Equivalent: Having the same value (e.g., 4 is equivalent to 8/2).

Estimate: To use prior knowledge to make an educated guess.

Fraction: A part of a whole.

Greater than (>): More than.

DOI: 10.4324/9781003238171-5

Height: A dimension measured from the bottom of an object to its top.

Inches: A U.S. customary unit used in linear measurement.

Length: A dimension measured from one end of an object to the other; how long an object is.

Less than (<): Not as much as.

Meterstick: A linear measurement tool used to measure lengths of up to one meter. It typically has markings for 100 centimeters. It is the metric equivalent of a yardstick. One meter is equal to 1.0936 yards.

Metric system: A system of measurement used by scientists and throughout most of the world that bases units on 10. It uses units such as millimeters, centimeters, and meters.

Model: A physical, conceptual, or mathematical simplification of an object or process.

One fourth: One of the parts when a whole is divided equally into four parts.

One half: One of the parts when a whole is divided equally into two parts.

One third: One of the parts when a whole is divided equally into three parts.

Perimeter: The length around the outside of an object.

Prediction: An educated guess.

Rectangle: A two-dimensional figure made up of four sides and four 90° angles.

Rectangular prism: A three-dimensional figure with six faces made up of rectangles. (Young children may picture a cereal box.)

Rounding: To change a more precise number to a more convenient, approximate number.

Ruler: A 12-inch-long device used for linear measurement. Rulers typically show 1/16 of an inch markings, and some rulers also show centimeter markings.

Scale model: A model in which the dimensions are in the same proportions as in the real object.

Segment: A portion of a line.

Tape measure: A flexible measuring device with linear measurement markings that is longer than a ruler or meterstick/yardstick.

Three-dimensional (3-D): A descriptor for an item that has a length, a width, and a height.

Trundle wheel: A measurement tool (consisting of a wheel and a handle) that is pushed along the ground to measure large distances. Each rotation of the wheel measures one meter.

Two-dimensional (2-D): A descriptor for an item that has a length and a width. It appears to be flat.

Unit: A quantity used as a standard of measurement; it represents a segment of a whole.

U.S. customary units: A system of measurement commonly used in the United States that uses units such as inches, feet, and yards.

Whole: The entirety of an object.

Width: A dimension measured from one side of an object to the other; how wide the object is.

Yardstick: A linear measurement tool that can measure up to one yard. It typically has markings for 36 inches (divided into 16ths).

Zero point: The starting point of a measurement.

90° angle: A right angle; where two perpendicular lines intersect. (Young children may think of it as a corner.)

Part Two: Lesson Plans

Lesson Plans

Lesson 1: Preassessment
Lesson 2: Models
Lesson 3: Dimensions
Lesson 4: Comparing and Ordering Objects
Lesson 5: Partitioning
Lesson 6: Comparing Length by Rearranging Parts (Decomposing and Recomposing)
Lesson 7: Linear Measurement: Measuring Length Using Nonstandard Units
Lesson 8: Linear Measurement: Measuring Distance Using Nonstandard Units
Lesson 9: Linear Measurement: Measuring Height Using Nonstandard Units
Lesson 10: Linear Measurement: Measuring Length Using Standard Units
Lesson 11: Linear Measurement: Appropriate Units and Tools
Lesson 12: Measuring Perimeter
Lesson 13: Postassessment

Lesson 1: Preassessment

Instructional Purpose

- To assess student knowledge and understanding of unit topics

Main Idea

- Objects with different attributes are measured in different ways (appropriate measurement).

Objective

The students will be able to:

- Demonstrate an understanding of models, problem solving, and measurement concepts (via preassessment).

Materials and Handouts

- Container with various sized objects, one for each table
- Same Height Activity (Handout 1A)
- Twice as Tall Activity (Handout 1B)
- Half as Tall Activity (Handout 1C)
- "Lifeguard Lucy" (a doll about 2" tall)
- Chapter 1 of *Dinosaurs Before Dark* (Magic Tree House series) by Mary Pope Osborne (Random House) or any other book with a picture of a tree house
- Paper
- Pencils

Activities

1. The unit preassessment is broken into three parts: math content, math processes, and overarching concept. Begin the assessment with the math content activity. When students are finished, divide the class into two groups. One group will meet with you to complete the math process assessment, while the others will work on their own to complete the overarching concept assessment. Switch groups when they have finished.
2. *Math content* (representation, measuring, estimation, comparing): Place a container with many classroom objects of various sizes at each table. Introduce the students to "Lifeguard Lucy" (a doll approximately 2" tall). Tell them she is 2 inches tall. Ask them to look in the container to find an object that is about the same height as Lucy. When they find an object, they should trace its shape on **Same Height Activity (Handout 1A)** and then return the object to the box. Allow 5 minutes for this activity. Next, ask the students to find something that is about twice as tall as Lucy and to trace its shape on **Twice as Tall Activity (Handout 1B)**. Allow 5 minutes for this activity. Repeat the activity a final time, asking them to trace items that are half as tall as Lucy on **Half as Tall Activity (Handout 1C)**. (Scoring guide: 1 point for each item that is about the same size as Lucy; 1 point for each item that is about twice as tall as Lucy; 1 point for each item that is half as tall as Lucy.)

DOI: 10.4324/9781003238171-7

3. *Math processes* (problem solving): Read to the students Chapter 1 from *Dinosaurs Before Dark*. Ask them to answer the following question: "If you had a big tree in your backyard and you wanted to build a tree house in it, what would you have to know before you built it?" Take notes of their responses or ask students to record their individual responses on paper, into a voice recorder, or through the use of a scribe (e.g., volunteer, aide, older student). (Scoring guide: 1 point for each different reasonable response.)
4. *Overarching concept* (models): Ask the students to draw a model of the school's playground, making it as accurate as possible. (Scoring guide: 1 point for each correct item; 1 point for each item that is in the correct location.)

Notes to Teacher

- Select items for the container that are easy for the students to trace so that you can quickly identify what the object is. Remind the students to trace the item in the direction that corresponds to the statement. For example, if the student selects a marker as being twice as tall as Lifeguard Lucy, he or she should trace the marker lying flat on the paper, rather than on its end, so the tracing will be twice as tall as Lucy.
- To assess the math content further, allow the students to decide how they want to compare Lifeguard Lucy to the other objects. Begin the activity by showing Lucy and then hiding her. A few students may be able to select items of a similar size simply by comparing them to the mental image they have of the doll. For students who are unable to do this, continually display Lucy so that they can select similar-sized objects by visual comparison. Students who find that task too difficult may actually need to manipulate Lucy to select items.
- Once the students have traced an object of similar size to Lucy, allow them an opportunity to self-assess by letting them actually compare the size of Lucy to the size of their drawings.

Name: ______________________________ Date: ______________

Same Height Activity (Handout 1A)

Directions: Trace an item from the container that is about the same height as Lifeguard Lucy.

Name: ______________________________ Date: ______________

Twice as Tall Activity (Handout 1B)

Directions: Trace an item from the container that is about twice as tall as Lifeguard Lucy.

Name: ______________________________ Date: ______________

Half as Tall Activity (Handout 1C)

Directions: Trace an item from the container that is about half as tall as Lifeguard Lucy.

Lesson 2: Models

Instructional Purpose

- To introduce the idea of models

Main Idea

- A model is a physical, conceptual, or mathematical simplification of an object or process.

Objectives

The students will be able to:

- Provide examples of models.
- Categorize lists of models.
- Identify nonexamples of models.
- Express generalizations about models.

Materials and Handouts

- Crayons
- Doll (Lifeguard Lucy)
- Drawing of a swimming pool from any book
- House blueprint
- Model car and corresponding photo of actual car
- Model of molecule
- Paper
- Small paper rectangle representing a bed
- Frayer Model of Vocabulary Development (Handout 2A)
- Need to Know Board (Teacher Resource 2A)
- Frayer Model of Vocabulary Development (Teacher Resource 2B)

Vocabulary

- Model
- Scale model

Activities

1. Introduce the idea of brainstorming to the students. Explain that when a group brainstorms, it comes up with as many ideas about the topic as it can. Students should not worry about whether their answers are right or wrong; the idea is simply to come up with many ideas. Practice brainstorming by asking the students what they would do if they found $10. Write their ideas on the board. (This is a fluency exercise, so all responses are valued.)
2. Read the following scenario aloud: *A swimming pool is about to be built in your neighborhood! The architect and construction workers need your help to figure out how to build it. The community has had several meetings to decide how to design the pool, but everyone seems to have different ideas about how deep the pool should be, what shape it should have, and what special features would be important. The adults cannot seem to agree on a design, so now the architect has decided*

DOI: 10.4324/9781003238171-8

to ask you for your ideas! Ask the students to brainstorm different suggestions they have for the architect. Write their ideas on the board. If you plan to do the *Building a Pool* extension, explain to the students that during this unit, they will actually be building a model of a pool for the architects to consider.

3. Next, tell the students that they are going to learn a process to help them think about problems (metacognitive planner). Use the **Need to Know Board (Teacher Resource 2A)** and complete it with the students' responses to the following questions:
   - What do we know?
   - What do we need to know?
   - How can we find out?

4. Explain that you just modeled a thinking process that the students can use any time they have a problem to which they need to find a solution. Ask the students to talk about the benefits of using this thinking process. Ask:
   - Did this process make the problem clearer?

5. Show the students several models (e.g., car, doll) and ask them what each represents. Why is it called a model? Talk about how models can also represent real things. Introduce the idea of scale. Show the students a model car and tell them that the car is 1/100th the size of an actual car. Show a photo of the actual car. Talk about the differences between a "life-sized" model and a "scale" model. Invite students to bring models from home to show the next day.
6. Show a drawing of a swimming pool in a book and talk about how the picture is a model that represents an actual pool. Ask the students whether there are any other pictures in the book that are models for real things. Ask:
   - Are models are always smaller than the real objects they represent?

7. Show the students a model of a molecule and explain that scientists sometimes create large models of very small things. Ask:
   - Why might scientists do this?

8. Show the students a house blueprint. Talk about how it is a smaller version of an actual house. Identify the scale of the blueprint. Discuss what the scale tells about the actual size of the house. Ask:
   - What would someone use a blueprint for?
   - Could they use a blueprint to test something out?

9. Show the students a small rectangle representing a bed. Tell them that it is the same scale as the blueprint. Ask:
   - What could they use the small bed for?

10. Talk to students about how they could test whether the actual bed would fit into an actual bedroom using the scale model and the blueprint. Have them compare the blueprint of the house to a blueprint the architect might draw for a swimming pool.
11. Divide the class into small groups of 3–4 students. Explain and assign roles to each student in the group: recorder, reporter, supporter (manages materials, keeps the group on task, encourages), and timekeeper.

12. Display a copy of the **Frayer Model of Vocabulary Development (Teacher Resource 2B)** on chart paper or on a document camera. Ask the students what the definition of a "model" is. Write their definition on the chart.
13. Discuss this definition: "A model is a physical, conceptual, or mathematical simplification of an object or process." Ask the students to compare and contrast the "official definition" with the class's definition. Ask:
    - How is your group's definition of model like this definition?
    - How is your group's definition of model different than this definition?
14. Give each group a copy of the **Frayer Model of Vocabulary Development (Handout 2A)** and have students put the definition in the appropriate section.
15. Have students work on the section titled "What a Model Is" to show what a model is or does. Ask groups to write down or draw what a model is in the appropriate section. Have reporters share group answers with the class.
16. Explain that there are many different types of models. Have student groups discuss examples of models. Ask groups to share responses with the class and then list them on the large group chart. Ask:
    - Are all of the listed items really models?
    - Why or why not?
    - What do the listed items represent?
    - What would someone use these models for?
17. Repeat the process, asking the students to give nonexamples of models, and then share responses. Ask:
    - What generalizations can you make about models?

Notes to Teacher

- Students may enjoy bringing a beach towel from home to sit on during various activities during the unit.
- As a prelude to future *Building a Pool* activities, tell the students that they will use the swimming pool model they drew in the assessment to help create a physical model of a swimming pool.

Assessment

- Have the students draw their own model of a swimming pool and explain why it is considered a model.

Extension

The following student activity can be used to extend the lesson.

- Have the students build a clay or Legos® model of various items.

Name: ______________________________ Date: ______________

Frayer Model of Vocabulary Development (Handout 2A)

Definition Write your class definition of "model."	**What a Model Is** Write or draw what a model is.
MODEL	
Examples Draw or write some examples of models.	**Nonexamples** Draw or write some nonexamples of models.

Need to Know Board (Teacher Resource 2A)

What do we know?	What do we need to know?	How can we find out?

Frayer Model of Vocabulary Development (Teacher Resource 2B)

Definition	**What a Model Is**
• A model is a physical, conceptual, or mathematical simplification of an object or process.	• A model serves as a representative of something. • When something is too big to have the real thing, we use a model.
Examples	**Nonexamples**
• Model cars • Dolls • Dollhouses	• A real car • A person • A real house

MODEL

Lesson 3: Dimensions

Instructional Purpose

- To introduce the ideas of dimensions

Main Ideas

- Objects with different attributes are measured in different ways (appropriate measurement).
- Items may be grouped by comparing and contrasting their attributes (classification).

Objectives

The students will be able to:

- Describe what the words "height," "depth," "length," and "width" refer to.
- Give examples of when to use the word "height" or "depth" to describe an object.
- Identify the characteristics of two-dimensional and three-dimensional objects using appropriate terminology.
- Compare two- and three-dimensional representations of objects.
- Give examples of two- and three-dimensional objects.
- Identify the similarities and differences between two- and three-dimensional objects.

Materials and Handouts

- Aquarium (or other large container to fill with water)
- Bag
- Blocks, dice, or other rectangular prisms
- Bookshelf (or other item to demonstrate inward depth measurement)
- Crayons
- Geoboards
- Paper
- Photos of above-ground and below-ground swimming pools
- Plate
- Play-Doh™ or clay
- Rectangular shapes of various sizes and colors cut from paper
- Sponge animal (the type that expands when water is added)
- Various containers (e.g., cup, trashcan, plastic containers)
- Water
- Handouts 3A–3G (for extension activity)
- ≋ Completed "pool" to show students
- ≋ Hot glue
- ≋ 3"x 5" sticky notes (two per student)
- ≋ 6-quart plastic container with lid (outside dimensions approximately 13" length x 8" width x 4.5"depth; one per student)
- ≋ 12" x 12" blue cardstock (one page per student)

DOI: 10.4324/9781003238171-9

Vocabulary

- Depth
- Height
- Length
- Rectangle
- Rectangular Prism
- Three-dimensional (3-D)
- Two-dimensional (2-D)
- Width

Activities

1. *Thinking About the Problem:* Read and discuss the following situation using the metacognitive planner discussed in the Notes to Teacher section. *The architects need to think about many measurements when they design a pool. Height, length, width, and depth are very important measurement ideas that the builders must understand before they can begin digging the hole for the swimming pool. What are some items you can think of at a swimming pool that are measured according to their height, length, width, and depth?*
2. Bring in an aquarium or other large container and let the children help fill it with water. Talk about the aquarium and the water within it. What could it be a model of? What terms could students use to describe how tall the aquarium is? Ask:
   - How could you characterize how much water is in the aquarium?
   - Would you ever refer to the height of the water?
   - When would you use one term versus the other?

   Explain that looking from the outside of the aquarium, you can see the height of the water, but looking from the top of the aquarium, you would measure the depth of the water.
3. When the students understand what height and depth mean, select containers from the classroom to which they could apply both terms (e.g., trash cans, cups, plastic containers) and ask the students to describe them in terms of their height and depth. Then talk about typical items outside of the classroom we refer to using the term "height" (e.g., people, buildings, trees) and depth (e.g., ocean, swimming pool, hole, a cut). Talk about a swimming pool and how a pool's depth is usually characterized by its "shallow end" and its "deep end."
4. Talk about how depth can also be measured horizontally inward from a surface, such as the depth of a bookshelf. Ask the students to look around the classroom to identify other items that may have horizontal depth measurements (e.g., a desk, a desk drawer, a cubby).
5. Put several pieces of paper cut out into rectangular shapes of different sizes into a bag. Add several blocks or rectangular prisms of different sizes to the bag. Have students pull out items, describe them, and group them as they see fit. Ask them why they grouped them as they did. Introduce the concept of two- and three-dimensional objects by discussing the ways in which the students grouped the items. Show them a rectangle and introduce the terminology "length" and "width." Point out several more rectangles and ask the students to help you identify the length and width.
6. Show the students a rectangular prism and ask them to talk about the differences between the prism and a rectangle. Have them point out the length and

width of the prism. Ask them what makes the prism different from the rectangle. Discuss the idea that the rectangular prism also has a height dimension.

7. Explain that the rectangle is a two-dimensional object because it is flat. It is characterized by only two dimensions: length and width. Contrast this with the rectangular prism. Discuss how students can measure it in three dimensions: length, width, and height; therefore, it is called a three-dimensional object. Point out that three-dimensional objects have a thickness to them.
8. Introduce the terminology "2-D" and "3-D" for two- and three-dimensional objects, respectively. On the board, make a chart of 2-D and 3-D characteristics. As the students discuss different characteristics or examples, write them on the board.
9. Show the students a flat sponge animal. Explain how it looks flat or two-dimensional. Place it on a plate and add water so that the animal expands (and becomes three-dimensional).
10. Explain that photographs or pictures of items may look flat, but are really models of three-dimensional items. Select a simple photo (such as one of a bus) and show them a clay model of it to demonstrate how they can make a three-dimensional model from a two-dimensional picture. Refer back to the pictures of the pool and ask the students to point out objects that are really three-dimensional.
11. Tell the students that they can model three-dimensional items in two dimensions by using a geoboard. Hold up a block or other simple three-dimensional item and demonstrate how they could model the shape on the geoboard. Using various three-dimensional objects, have the students practice representing the item in two dimensions. Now show the students a new shape on the geoboard and ask them what three-dimensional item it might represent.

Assessment

- Ask the students to change a two-dimensional model into a three-dimensional model or vice versa. Allow them to use any material in the classroom. For example, they could look at a picture (2-D) and make a clay model of it (3-D) or look at an object (3-D) and draw a picture of it (2-D). Ask them to tell how a model is different from what it represents and why they might want to have a model. Ask them to tell whether their representation is "life-sized" or "scale" and to explain the difference.

Notes to Teacher

- Each lesson begins with a *Thinking About the Problem* section to encourage the students to think carefully about the process of solving a problem. Read the short scenario and allow the students to think about how they might solve the problem. Create a "Need to Know" board to use as a metacognitive planner and complete it with the students' responses to the following questions:
    - What do we know?
    - What do we need to know?
    - How can we find out?

  Revisit the board at the end of the lesson to see whether students were able to solve the problem.
- Students may become confused about which dimension is the length and which is the width. Explain that the length normally refers to the longer side, rather than the direction that side is facing. For example, you might hold a piece

of notebook paper up vertically (portrait view) and point out the length dimension along the side of the paper, and then turn the paper horizontally (landscape view) to show that now the length is along the top (or bottom) of the paper.

- It is less satisfactory to use pictures of 3-D objects than real 3-D objects. You might consider taking a digital photo of an object in your classroom and then pointing out to the students that a picture, although 2-D, can represent a 3-D object.

Extension

- Have the students cut out a two-dimensional net of a shape (such as a cube) and then fold it into a three-dimensional object **(Handouts 3A, 3B, 3C, 3D, 3E, 3F, and 3G)**.
- Tell the students that they will be changing a two-dimensional model of a swimming pool like the one they created yesterday into a three-dimensional model. Talk about the utility of using a three-dimensional model (e.g., a three-dimensional model can hold water). Show them a completed model of the swimming pool using a plastic container and foam core board. (See instructions in Part Three.)
- Pre-cut a piece of blue cardstock that will fit lengthwise inside each plastic container, angling from the bottom of the container (deep end) to about the middle of the container's height (shallow end). This represents the bottom of the pool. For a more realistic pool, cut the plastic container lid into the same shape and hot glue it (prior to class) to the container so that the students can eventually fill the pool with water. Give each student a plastic container and have him or her identify and label the shallow end and deep end of the pool using sticky notes inside of the plastic box.

Name: ______________________________ Date: ____________

Net of a Cube (Handout 3A)

Directions: Cut along the solid outside line. Fold along the dotted lines. What 3-D figure did you make?

Name: ______________________________ Date: ______________

Net of a Cylinder (Handout 3B)

Directions: Cut along the solid outside line. Fold along the dotted lines. What 3-D figure did you make?

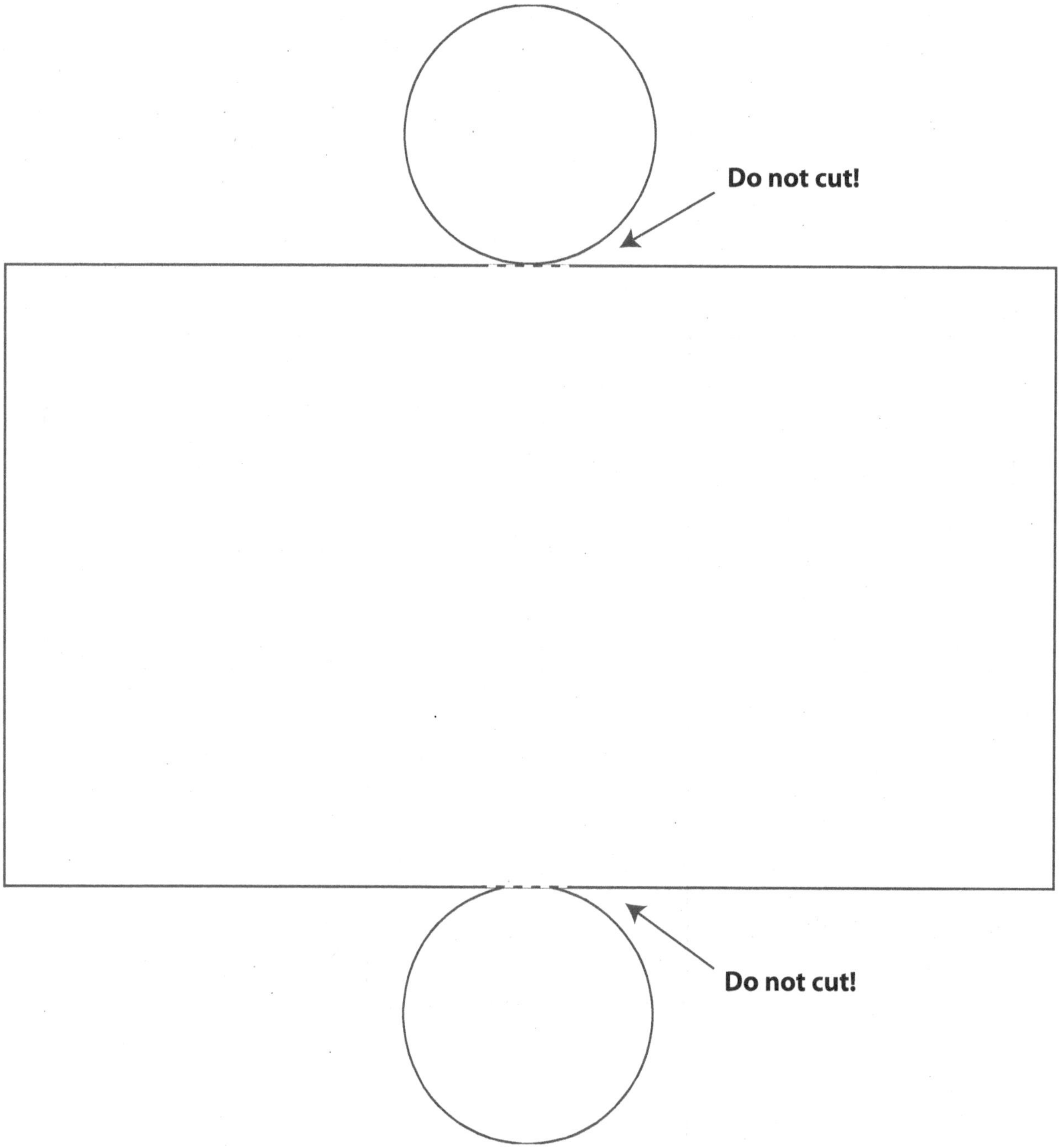

Name: ______________________________ Date: ______________

Net of a Cone (Handout 3C)

Directions: Cut along the solid outside line. Fold along the dotted lines. What 3-D figure did you make?

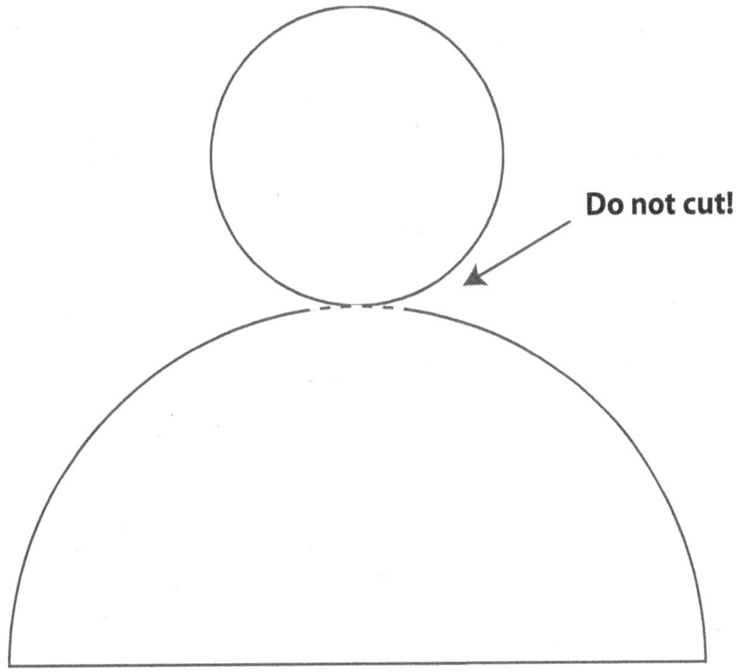

Name: ______________________________ Date: ______________

Net of a Square Pyramid (Handout 3D)

Directions: Cut along the solid outside line. Fold along the dotted lines. What 3-D figure did you make?

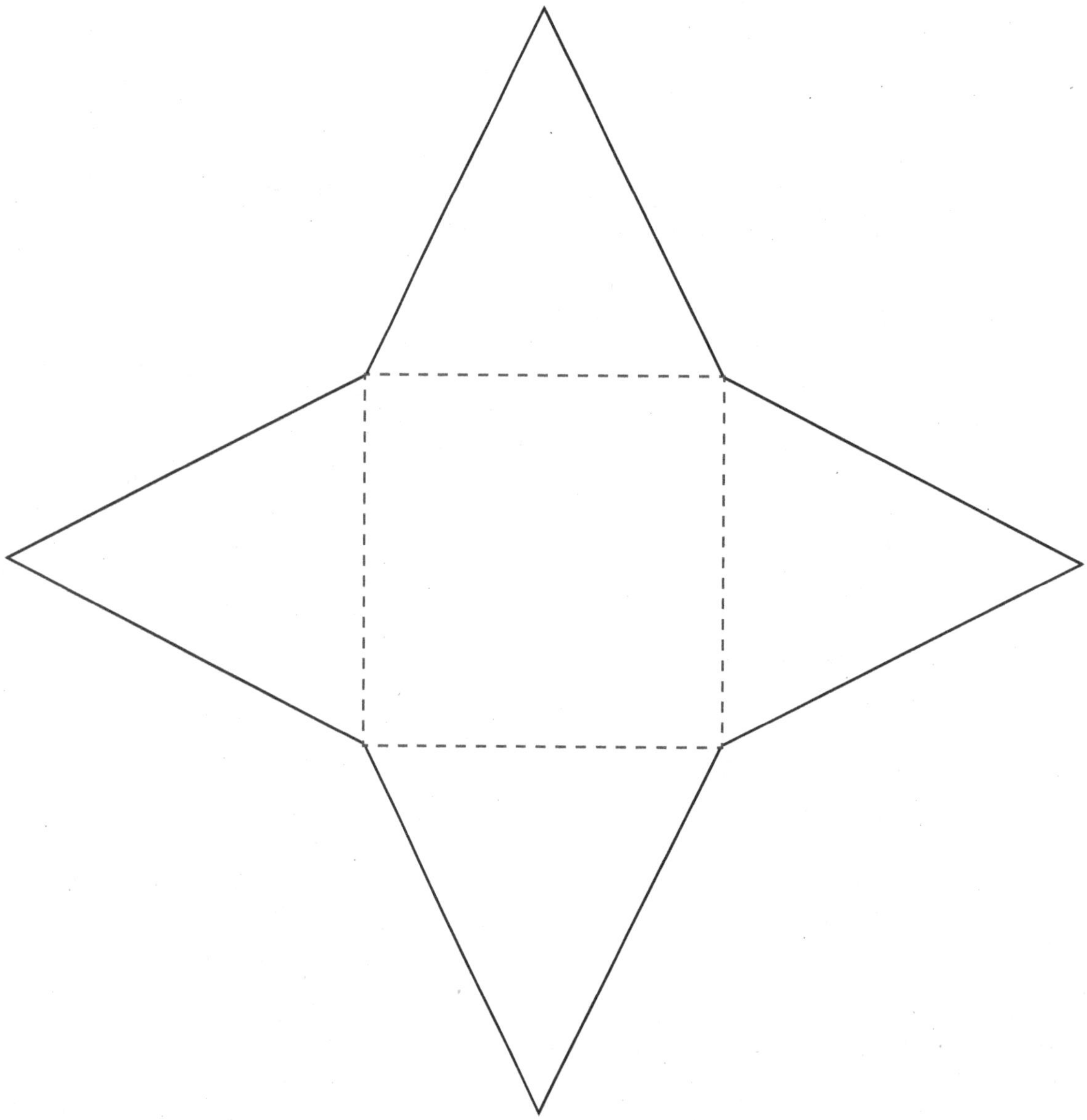

Name: ______________________________ Date: ______________

Net of a Triangular Pyramid (Handout 3E)

Directions: Cut along the solid outside line. Fold along the dotted lines. What 3-D figure did you make?

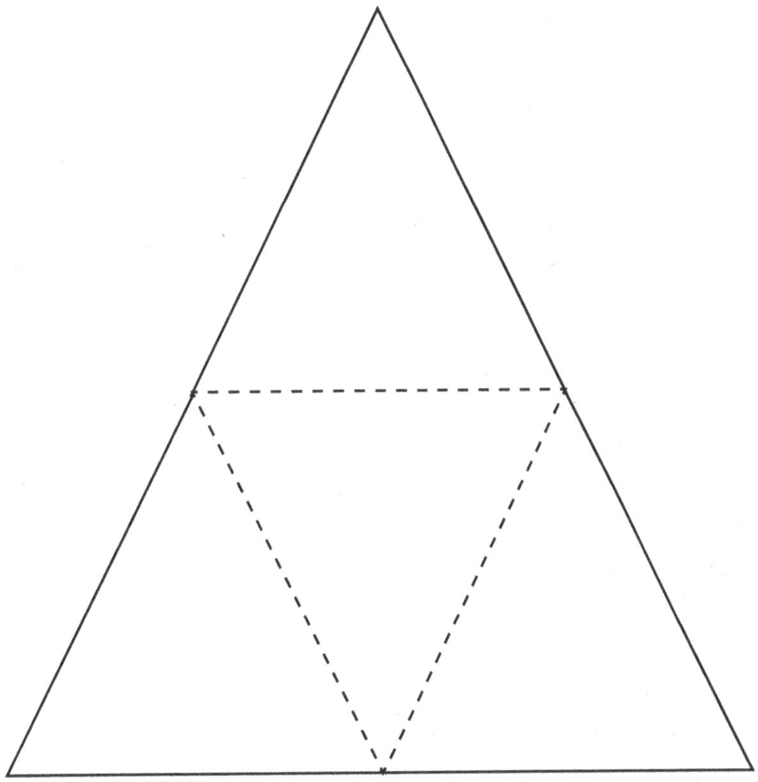

Name: ______________________________ Date: ______________

Net of a Rectangular Prism (Handout 3F)

Directions: Cut along the solid outside line. Fold along the dotted lines. What 3-D figure did you make?

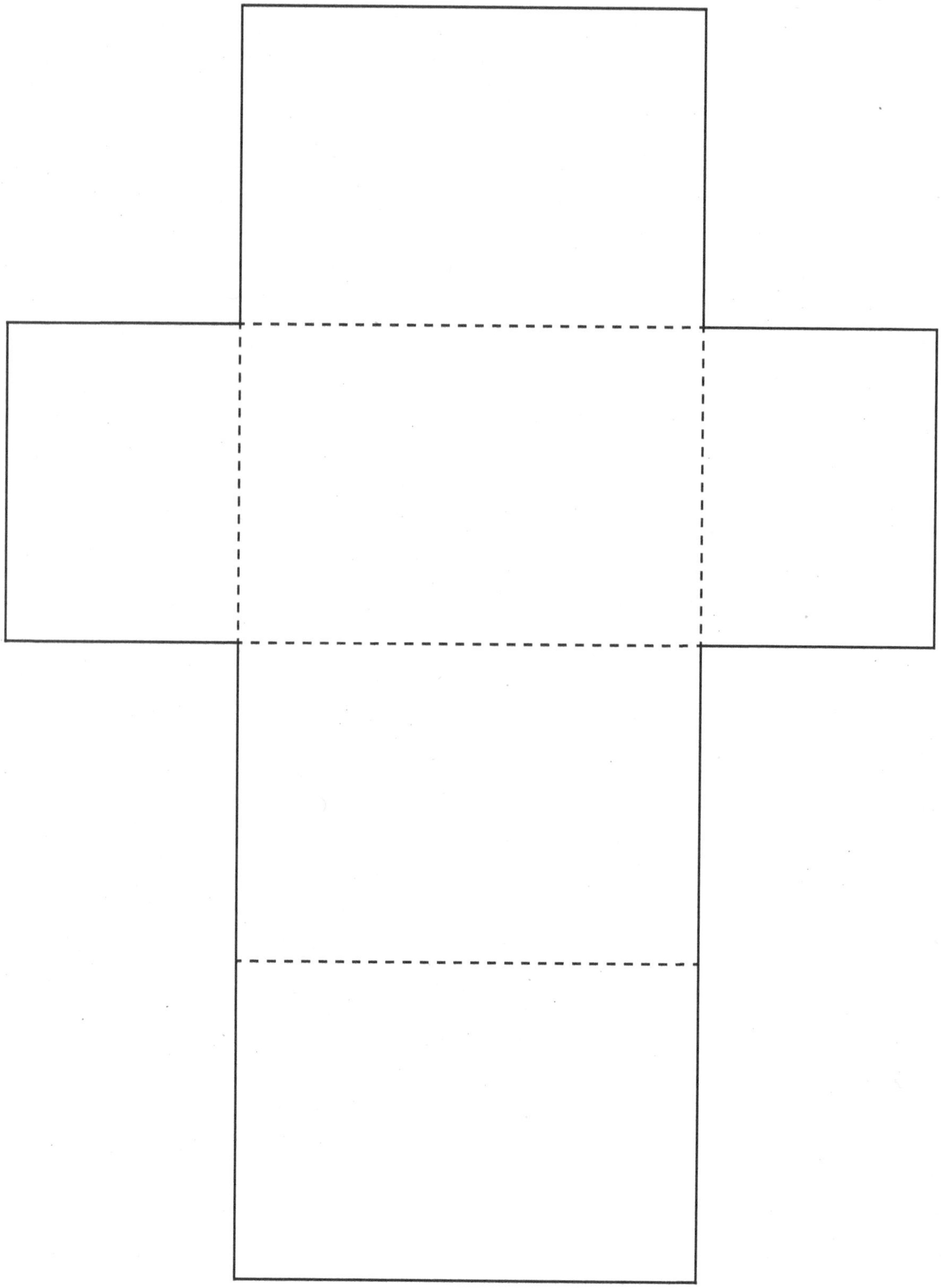

Name: ______________________________ Date: ______________

Net of a Triangular Prism (Handout 3G)

Directions: Cut along the solid outside line. Fold along the dotted lines. What 3-D figure did you make?

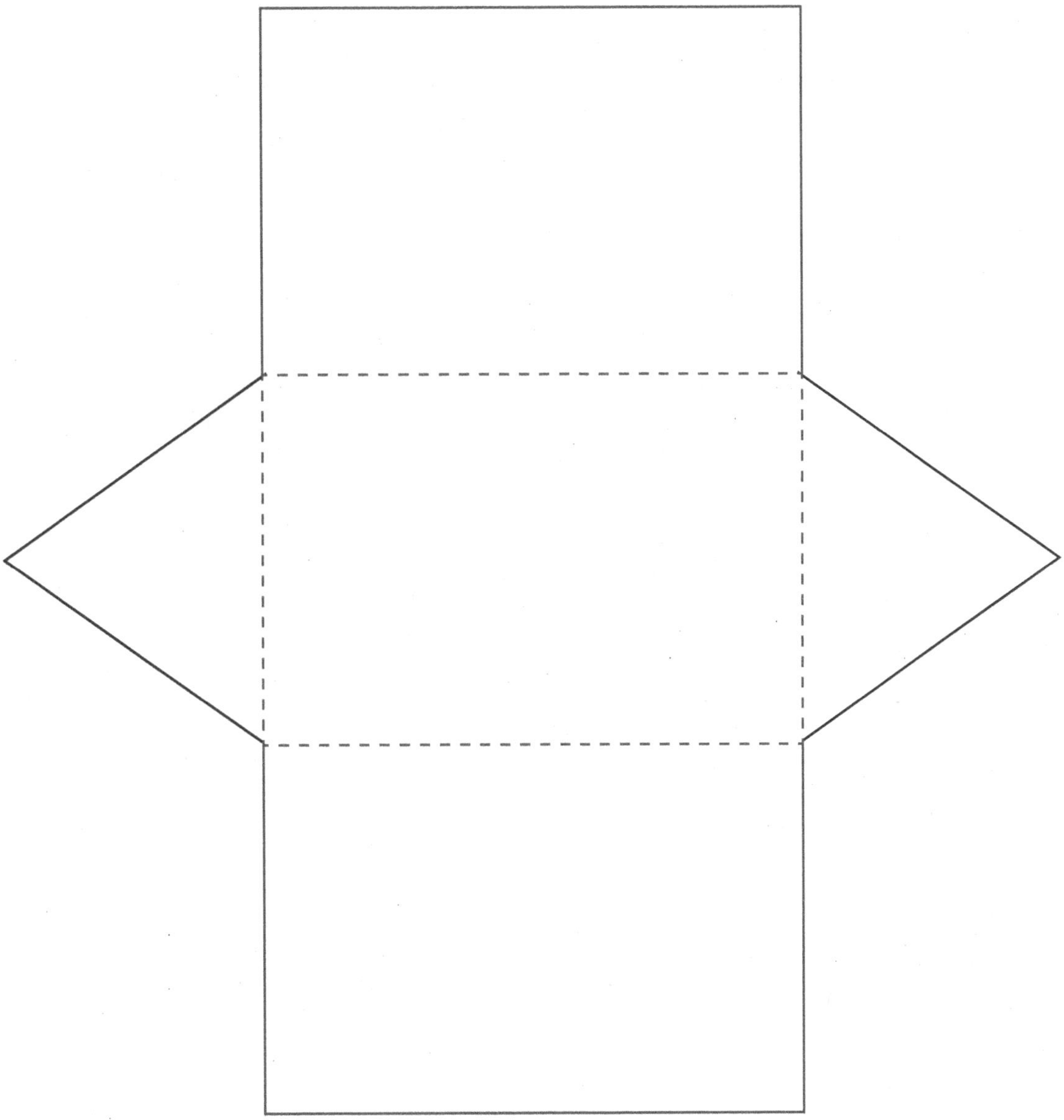

Lesson 4: Comparing and Ordering Objects

Instructional Purpose

- To compare and order objects by length

Main Ideas

- An item remains the same length even when placed in a different position (conservation).
- Knowing the relationship between one item and a second item, and between the second item and a third item, one may deduce the relationship between the first item and third item can be deduced (transitivity).

Objectives

The students will be able to:

- Compare and order three or more objects according to length using direct and indirect comparison.
- Compare objects to each another using appropriate terminology (greater than, less than, equal to).
- Compare and order objects that are not facing in the same direction.

Materials

- Construction paper of several colors
- Craft sticks cut to three slightly different lengths
- Crayons
- Masking tape
- Scissors
- Wide fabric ribbons cut so that the colors from shortest to longest are red, white, blue (one set per student; add two additional color ribbons if doing the extension activity)

Vocabulary

- Equal to (=)
- Greater than (>)
- Less than (<)

Activities

1. *Thinking About the Problem:* Read and discuss the following situation using the metacognitive planner discussed in the Notes to Teacher section. *The workers are ready to build the locker room. They have three stacks of lumber. The boards in the first stack are shorter than the second stack. The boards in the second stack are shorter than the third stack. How does the length of the boards in the third stack compare to the length of the boards in the first stack? How can the workers determine this answer without directly measuring the stacks?*

DOI: 10.4324/9781003238171-10

2. Ask the students to stand up. Call the shortest person to the front of the room. Call the next shortest student to the front of the room. Compare their heights. Tell the students that they are going to line up in order from shortest to tallest by height. Discuss what it means to put something in order. Are things only in order from shortest to tallest, or can "in order" also refer to tallest to shortest? Discuss the importance of knowing the direction in which we are trying to order.
3. Introduce the terminology (greater than, less than, and equal to) and the terms' related symbols. Write them on the board. Go around the classroom and compare various objects until the students are familiar with using the terminology. For example, *The height of the desk is less than the height of the bookcase.*
4. Distribute construction paper of various colors and tell the students that you want them to make the best two-dimensional models they can of their shoes. Discuss how they might do this. (Students should come up with the idea of tracing around their feet). Allow them time to decorate their "footprints," making sure they write their names on the fronts. Have them cut out the footprints, and then ask them to tape them to the board randomly.
5. Ask the students to categorize the footprints in as many different ways as possible to encourage fluency and flexibility. Have students discuss the rationale of their categorization.
6. Tell the students that you want to put the footprints in order from shortest to longest (footprints "A" to "Z"). Ask the students what strategy they might use to do this. Begin by selecting two footprints that are not facing the same direction. Ask the students how they would compare them. Bring out the point that although the footprints may be facing different directions, the length of them does not change.
7. Demonstrate how to compare the footprints by placing them vertically, side-by-side, on the board. Call on students to help you place the footprints in order by direct comparison. As they compare the footprints, ask them to talk about each one using mathematical terminology (e.g., the length of Jennie's footprint is greater than the length of Matt's footprint).
8. Ask the students how else they might compare the footprints (by width). Order the footprints by width and talk about terms such as "wide" and "narrow."
9. Mix up the footprints and select two at random (G and K) and compare them. Write on the board, "length of G < length of K." Select a shorter footprint (B) and compare it to footprint G and again write the relationship on the board. Now ask the students whether footprint B or footprint K is longer. Write the relationship between B and K on the board and encourage the students to talk about why they think one is longer than the other.
10. Try this with several other footprints to help the students understand that they can use what they know about the relationship between two sets of footprints (G and K, G and B) to determine the relationship between another set (B and K). Ask them to predict how many hand spans would equal a footprint. How many footprints equal an arm's length? Encourage them to make comparisons with other parts of their bodies.
11. Allow the students to work in groups of three. Tell them they are going to model the lumber problem using craft sticks. Number each group member and ask that student to close his or her eyes. Place a craft stick in each student's hand, ensuring that Student 1 receives the craft stick that is the middle length, Student 2 receives the long stick, and Student 3 receives the short stick. Tell the students to hide their craft sticks behind their backs and to open their eyes. Ask Student 1 to hold his or her stick next to Student 2's stick and to compare their lengths

using the mathematical terminology on the board. When they have determined which is longer, Student 2 should hide his or her stick again. Ask Student 1 to compare his or her stick to that of Student 3 and again talk about the size relationship using mathematical terminology. When they have determined which is longer, Students 1 and 3 should hide their sticks. Without letting the students look at the sticks or directly measure them, ask the group to talk about the size relationship between Sticks 2 and 3. Ask them how they know their answer is correct. Once they have explained their rationale, ask them to place the sticks in order, shortest to tallest. Ask:

- How can you use the activity you just did to help solve the lumber problem at the beginning of the lesson?

Assessment

- Distribute a set of three ribbons of different lengths to each student (from shortest to longest, they should be red, white, and blue). Have them immediately put away the ribbons so they cannot directly compare them. Ask them to pull out the white and blue ribbons and place them next to each other to determine which is longer. Have them write down the relationship (length of white < length of blue). Tell them to put the blue ribbon away and pull out the red ribbon. Have them compare the red and white ribbons to determine which is longer. Have them write down the relationship (length of red < length of white). Without allowing them to measure, ask the students to write down the relationship between the red and blue ribbon (length of red < length of blue). Ask:
  - How do you know?
  - What other relationships between the different ribbons do you know?
  - How do you know they are correct?

Notes to Teacher

- This lesson begins with a *Thinking About the Problem* activity to encourage the students to carefully think about the process of solving a problem. Read the short scenario and allow the students to think about how they might solve the problem. Create a "Need to Know" board to use as a metacognitive planner and complete it with the students' responses to the following questions:
  - What do we know?
  - What do we need to know?
  - How can we find out?

  Revisit the board at the end of the lesson to see whether they were able to solve the problem.
- The ability to deduce transitivity (if one knows the relationship between one item and a second item, and between the second item and a third item, the relationship between the first item and third item can be deduced) occurs in children prior to the logic of unit iteration (Battista, 2006).
- Once the students grasp the idea of "$A < B$," encourage them to discuss what other conclusions they might draw from this mathematical statement ($B > A$; $A \neq B$).
- Students may enjoy working on logic problems when they complete an activity. Consider creating a collection of such problems for them to solve at their leisure. For example, ask the students to solve the following logic problem: Gabi is shorter than Dave, but taller than Barb. Who is taller, Dave or Barb? How do you know?

Extension

The following student activities can be used to extend the lesson.

- For added complexity, have the students indirectly compare four or five ribbons of different lengths. Ask them what relationships they can determine and how they know they are correct.
- Have the students choose their own items for their partners to compare and order.

Lesson 5: Partitioning

Instructional Purpose

- To visualize how whole objects can be partitioned

Main Ideas

- The length of an object can be divided into equal-sized units (partitioning).
- Sets of items may look different, but represent the same amount of equivalence.

Objectives

The students will be able to:

- Partition objects into equal parts.
- Recognize that the equal parts can be put together to create a whole.

Materials

- Blue bond paper (8.5" x 11")
- Pipe cleaner
- Strips of paper (adding machine paper works well)
- Unifix™ cubes (12 per student)
- ≈ Markers
- ≈ Students' plastic "pools"

Vocabulary

- Unit
- Whole

Activities

1. *Thinking About the Problem*: Read and discuss the following situation using the metacognitive planner discussed in the Notes to Teacher section. *The builders want the pool to have six lanes. How can they decide how wide to make each lane?*
2. Introduce the concept of partitioning by showing the students a piece of pipe cleaner. Fold it into quarters and then straighten it back out, marking where the quarters were. Talk about how students can imagine the length of an object divided into equal pieces.
3. Hand the students long strips of paper and talk about each strip being one whole length. Direct the students as they fold the lengths into eighths and then talk about how each unit is equal. Look around the classroom and have students talk about how they could physically partition certain items.
4. Give the students 12 Unifix™ cubes each. Ask them to stack up the cubes. Discuss how the stack makes up one whole length. Ask the students how they could divide the stack into pieces of the smallest unit possible (12 one-piece segments).
5. Next, ask the students how they could divide the stack equally using larger units. Once they discover they can divide the stack into six two-piece segments, have them do so by putting two blue pieces together to represent a unit, then two

DOI: 10.4324/9781003238171-11

white pieces to represent another unit, and so forth until they have a stack of 12. (Students can trade pieces or use additional pieces so they have enough colors.)

6. Ask them if there is another way they could make equal segments. Repeat this process until students have made four three-piece segments, three four-piece segments, two six-piece segments, and one 12-piece segment. Make sure the students create each segment using all of the same color Unifix™ cubes to show the boundaries of that segment.
7. Show the different stacks of 12 and ask the students to compare and contrast them. Do they all represent the same total height? How do students know this? Discuss the reasons why students might decide to divide something into four equal parts instead of six equal parts.

Assessment

- Refer the students back to the *Thinking About the Problem* situation. Give each student a piece of blue paper and explain that this represents a two-dimensional model of a three-dimensional swimming pool. Tell students that you want to divide the pool into six equal lanes. Ask them to think about different ways they could divide the pool into lanes using terms such as "length" and "width." Make a class list. Tell the students to divide the pool and draw lines down the length of the pool to show how they would make the lanes equal using a method from the list or one of their own.

Notes to Teacher

- This lesson begins with a *Thinking About the Problem* activity to encourage the students to carefully think about the process of solving a problem. Read the short scenario and allow the students to think about how they might solve the problem. Create a "Need to Know" board to use as a metacognitive planner and complete it with the students' responses to the following questions:
  - o What do we know?
  - o What do we need to know?
  - o How can we find out?

  Revisit the board at the end of the lesson to see whether students were able to solve the problem. While discussing the problem, do not actually demonstrate how to divide the lanes, as they will be doing this as part of their assessment.

Extension

The following student activities can be used to extend the lesson.

- This lesson can easily be extended to talk about the relationships between various units. When the students initially fold the paper into eighths, you might have a discussion about the relationships between the different segments. For example, ask them how many eighths make up a fourth and how many make up a half. Similarly, a natural outgrowth from creating the Unifix™ towers would be a discussion about the relationships between twelfths, sixths, fourths, and so on.
- This lesson could also lead into a discussion about factors. Ask the students to make units of five Unifix™ cubes and discuss why they cannot build a stack of 12. Have the students come up with other lengths that they could evenly partition.

- Rather than using a full sheet of paper for the assessment, cut the paper to the width of the plastic container. After the students have marked their six lanes on the paper, help them to use it as a template to mark lane line locations at each end of their plastic containers with a marker.

Lesson 6: Comparing Length by Rearranging Parts (Decomposing and Recomposing)

Instructional Purpose

- To compare length by repeating smaller units

Main Ideas

- The length of an object can be divided into equal-sized units (partitioning).
- The length of a larger unit may be made up of repeating smaller units (unit iteration).

Objectives

The students will be able to:

- Compare objects by decomposing parts.
- Compare objects by recomposing parts.
- Model a simple process by drawing its path.

Materials and Handouts

- Ball
- Crazy Swimmer Activity (Handout 6)
- Pipe cleaner (12" length)
- Plastic straws cut into 2-inch lengths (20 segments per student)
- Pipe Cleaner Model (Teacher Resource 6A)
- Comparing Pipe Cleaner Lengths (Teacher Resource 6B)
- Crazy Swimmer Activity (Teacher Resource 6C)

Vocabulary

- Segment
- 90° angle

Activities

1. *Thinking About the Problem:* Read and discuss the following situation using the metacognitive planner discussed in the Notes to Teacher section. *Before the builders pour the concrete for the swimming pool, they need to lay pipe. The pipe has lots of twists and turns, but they need to determine the total length to make sure they have enough. How can they decide how long the pipe needs to be?*
2. Introduce the lesson by showing the students two *unequal* lengths of pipe cleaner bent into various 90° angles as shown in **Teacher Resources 6A** and **6B**. Make each segment between bends one or two "units" long. Ask the students which length of pipe cleaner is longer, reminding them of how they learned to divide things into equal units. Ask:
    - What criteria did you use to decide one was longer than the other?

DOI: 10.4324/9781003238171-12

3. Draw the shapes of the pipe cleaners on the board, making a dot at the end of each segment. Talk about how these drawings are models of the pipe cleaners. Ask the students which pipe cleaner is longer based on the drawings. Talk about how students could straighten each pipe cleaner and compare their lengths. Draw arrows on the board to show them how they could do this as shown in **Pipe Cleaner Model (Teacher Resource 6A)**.
4. Ask the students if there is another way in which they might be able to compare the two lengths. On the board, demonstrate how they could match each unit of the two pipe cleaners to determine which has a longer length. Color each segment a different color and draw arrows between the corresponding units to demonstrate as shown in **Pipe Cleaner Lengths (Teacher Resource 6B)**.
5. Spread the students around the classroom and provide each student with 20 plastic straw segments. Have each student make a path with several 90° turns in it using 10 segments. Now, ask the students to make another path of a different design with the remaining 10 segments. Ask them to talk about the lengths of their two paths. Since the paths look different, how do students know they are the same length?
6. Inform the students that you are now going to model a process. Roll a ball so that it moves across the floor in a crooked path. Have the students watch its path. Ask:
   - Did it go straight?
   - Did its path go to the right or left?

   Ask the students whether they could somehow model the path it took.
7. Discuss how they can model the movement of an item by drawing the path. Demonstrate on the board. Summarize with a discussion of the following generalization: Real things and processes can be represented by pictures, drawings, diagrams, objects, or actions.

Assessment

- Tell the students that two swimmers were very confused during a race, and instead of swimming in a straight line, they swam along a crazy path. Distribute the **Crazy Swimmer Activity (Handout 6)**. The students' task is to figure out which swimmer swam further. Do not allow them to use any tools to measure the lines. Have them draw arrows to demonstrate their strategy. Use **Crazy Swimmer Activity (Teacher Resource 6C)** to review student responses.

Notes to Teacher

- Each lesson begins with a *Thinking About the Problem* activity to encourage the students to carefully think about the process of solving a problem. Read the short scenario and allow the students to think about how they might solve the problem. Create a "Need to Know" board to use as a metacognitive planner and complete it with the students' responses to the following questions:
   - o What do we know?
   - o What do we need to know?
   - o How can we find out?

   Revisit the board at the end of the lesson to see whether they were able to solve the problem.

- The concept of length can be confusing to students when twists and turns are involved. Does length refer to the straight-line distance between endpoints regardless of the turns in between, or does it refer to the entire distance accounting for each turn? It may be helpful to explain to the students that mathematically, they account for the entire distance, including the turns, just like they would if they were taking a trip in the car. (In science, we call the endpoint-to-endpoint distance "displacement" and the actual path traveled "distance.")

Extension

The following student activity can be used to extend the lesson.

- Bring an ant farm into class and have the students compare the lengths of the different paths the ants have made.

Name: ______________________________ Date: ________________

Crazy Swimmer Activity (Handout 6)

Directions: Figure out which swimmer swam further. Draw arrows to show your reasons.

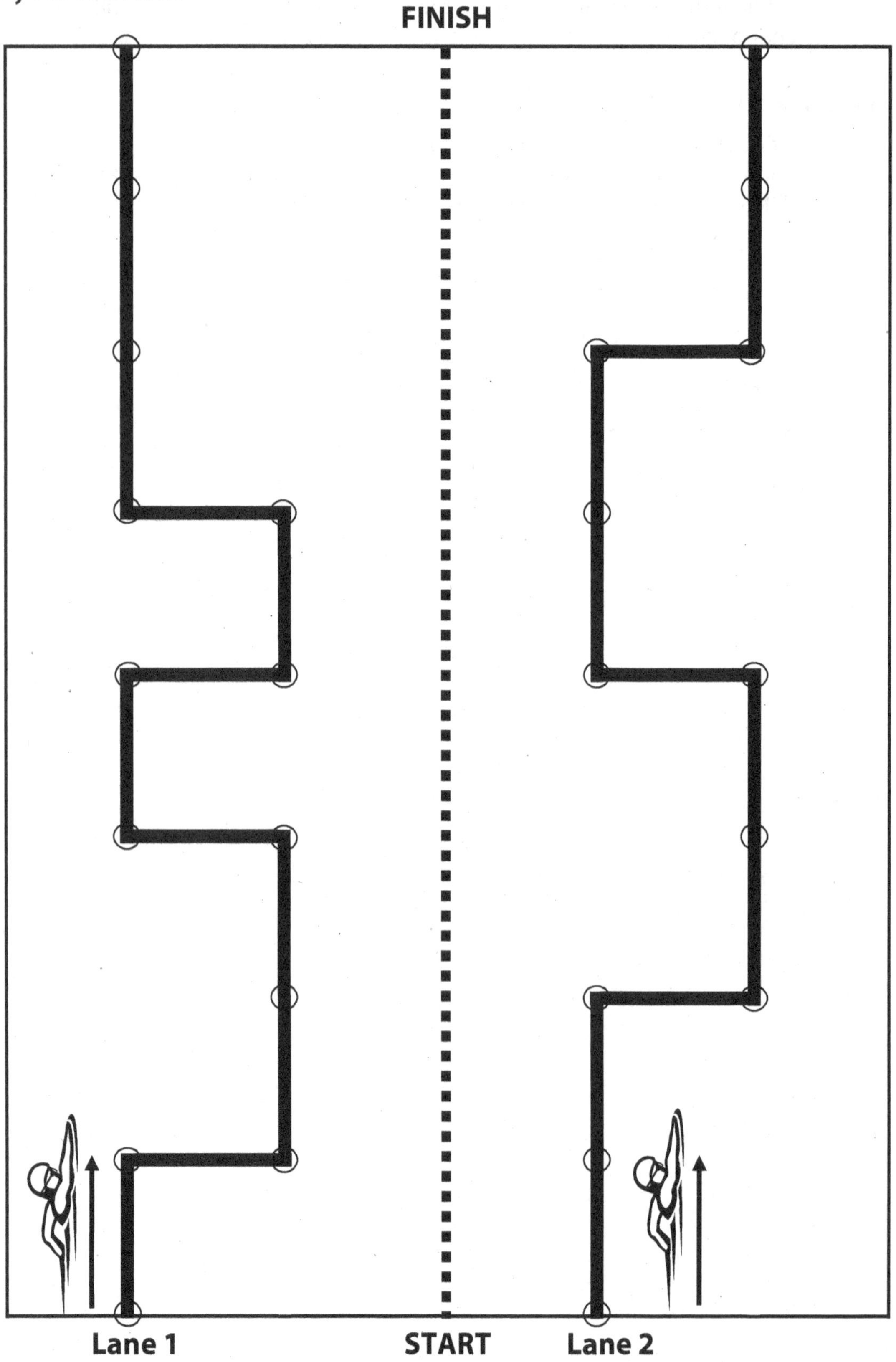

Pipe Cleaner Model (Teacher Resource 6A)

Pipe cleaner 1

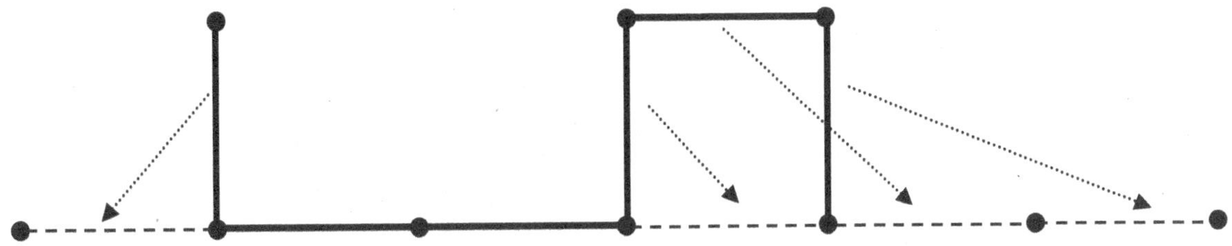

Pipe cleaner 2

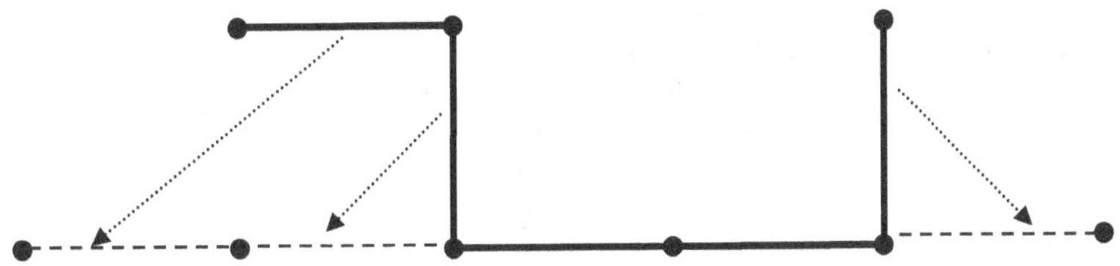

Adapted from Battista (2006).

Comparing Pipe Cleaner Lengths (Teacher Resource 6B)

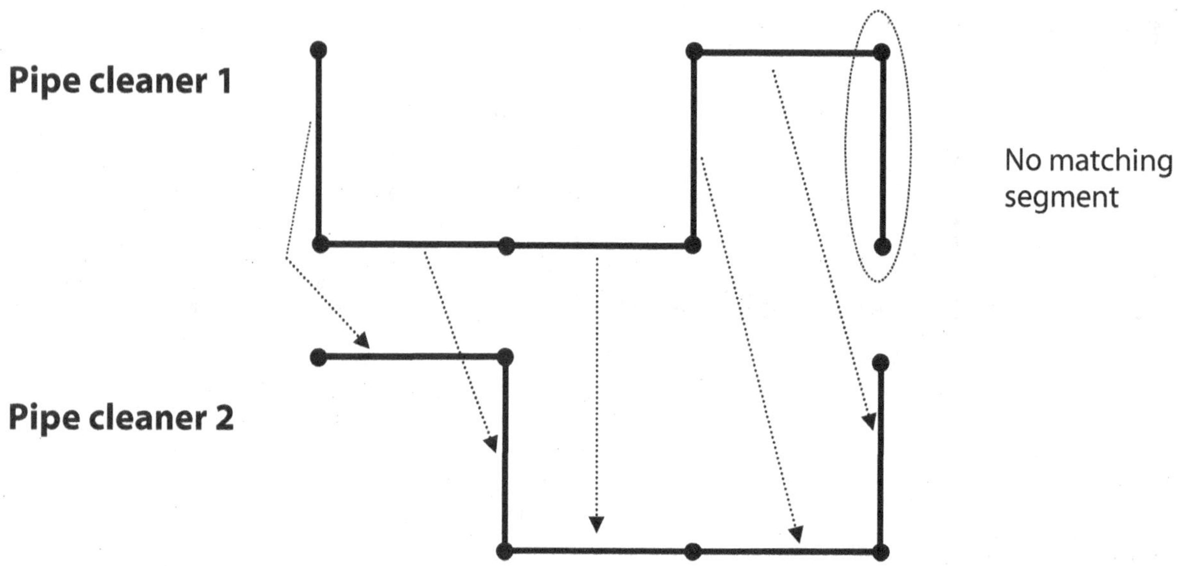

Adapted from Battista (2006).

Crazy Swimmer Activity (Teacher Resource 6C)

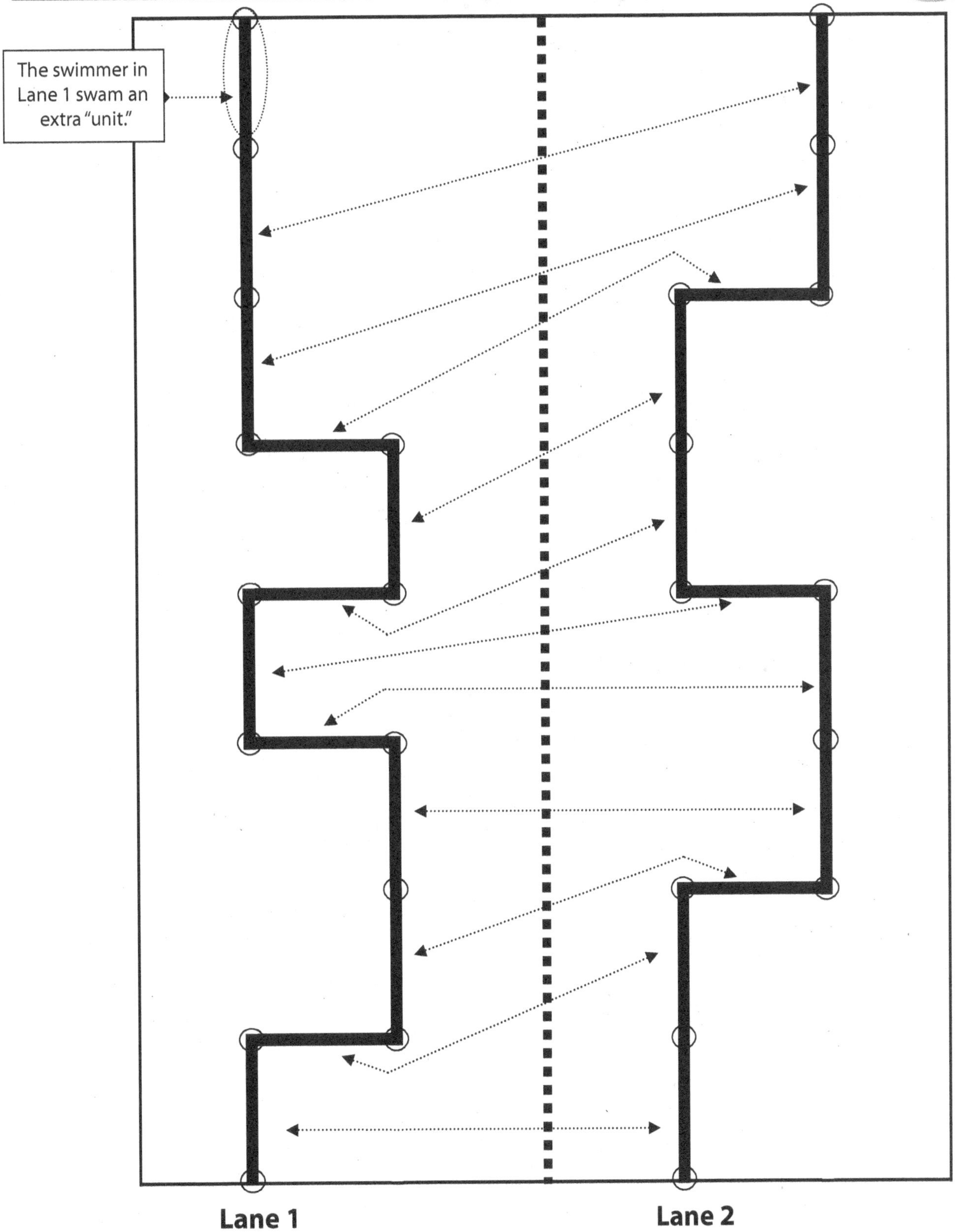

Adapted from Battista (2006).

Lesson 7: Linear Measurement: Measuring Length Using Nonstandard Units

Instructional Purpose

- To explore the fundamentals of accurate measurement

Main Ideas

- Accurate measurements require identical units, precise starting and ending points, no gaps or overlaps in coverage, and partitioning of leftover (non-whole) units (measurement accuracy).
- The length of an object can be divided into equal-sized units (partitioning).
- The length of a larger unit may be made up of repeating smaller units (unit iteration).
- The larger the unit of measure, the smaller the number of units needed to measure a particular object; the smaller the unit of measure, the larger the number of units needed to measure that same object (inverse relationship between size of units and number of units needed).
- Sometimes a close approximation of a number is accurate enough (rounding).
- Sets of items may look different, but represent the same amount (equivalence).

Objectives

The students will be able to:

- Identify the zero point (starting point) and endpoint of a measurement.
- Demonstrate measuring using nonstandard materials with no gaps or overlaps.
- Characterize "leftover" units by rounding using words and phrases such as "almost" or "a little more than."
- Explain that different units, such as hand spans and footsteps, may be used to measure the same things.
- Explain why units need to be identical within a measurement (e.g., can't use foot, then hand).
- Demonstrate equivalent ways of measuring (e.g., 3 footsteps = 5 hand spans).

Materials and Handouts

- Blue painter's tape or masking tape
- Index cards
- *Math Counts: Length* by Henry Pluckrose (Children's Press)
- Paper clips
- Ribbon (cut into 6" lengths)
- 8.5" x 11" green cardstock (five pages per student)
- Stapler or clear tape

Vocabulary

- Endpoint

DOI: 10.4324/9781003238171-13

- Equivalent
- Prediction
- Rounding
- Zero point

Activities

1. *Thinking About the Problem:* Read and discuss the following situation using the metacognitive planner discussed in the Notes to Teacher section. *The builders need to decide how long to make the pool. One worker wants to make the pool 100 steps long and another builder wants to make it 50 board-lengths long. How can we decide which will make the longer pool?*
2. Introduce the concept of linear measurement by giving the students the following scenario: *You are sitting on the edge of the pool. Your friend is standing in the middle of the pool. He says he can beat you to the other side. Is it a fair race? Why or why not?* Introduce the idea of starting points and ending points. Talk about how they can measure "how far" (distance) using length.
3. Hand the students index cards and ask them to measure their desks. Record their measurements on a chart (e.g., on the blackboard), with students' names in the left column and their measurements in the right column. Talk about the similarities and differences in student answers. Did it matter whether a student measured using the short side of the index card or the long side? Discuss the relationship between the length of the measuring object and the number of times it was used to measure the desk. Ask if there are other items students could have used to measure the desk. For example, would it take more or fewer paper clips to measure the desk?
4. Let the students measure the desk using paper clips to decide whether an index card or paper clip is easier to use. Ask them if they can make a rule to describe the relationship between the size of unit of measure and the number of units required.
5. Using blue painter's tape or masking tape, make a model of a swimming pool (about 10 feet long) on the floor. Have the students walk along the edge of the pool to see how many footsteps it is. Note where students start (zero point), where they end (endpoint), whether there are any gaps or overlaps, and what they do with the leftover units (partitioning). Have the students write their measurements (by footsteps) in a chart. Discuss the variations in measurements with the goal of having the students arrive at the idea that they need to start at the same point, end at the same point, and connect their footsteps without gaps or overlaps. Discuss how they can characterize the leftover units using rounding ("almost 12").
6. Once the students understand the idea of having accurate starting and ending points and no gaps or overlaps in their footsteps, have them predict how many footsteps the length of the pool really is. Write their predictions on the board. Have them measure the length of the pool again and record their new measurements on the chart. Did everyone get the same answer? Discuss the possible reasons for the different answers with the goal of having students realize that the size of a person's foot is related to the number of footsteps it took.
7. Place several "baby pool" models (smaller taped outlines) around the classroom. Talk about items students could use to measure the pools. Could students use several different items at the same time to measure the pools? Discuss the idea that once they start measuring, they need to keep the same measurement tool so that the units remain the same. Allow the students to select various items

from the classroom to measure the length of the pools, ensuring they start and end at the same point and do not have any gaps or overlaps. As they measure the pools, they should add their "unit" and measurement to the chart. Help them to characterize their leftover units. What generalizations can the students make? Introduce the concept of equivalence by comparing two of the measurements (16 pencils = 20 craft sticks). Have the students think of as many equivalent measurements as they can.

8. Introduce the idea of moving the starting and ending points to different locations by having students measure the height of the middle shelf of a bookshelf. Does the starting point always correspond to where the item begins? Model the bookshelf by drawing a picture of it on the board. Use an arrow to demonstrate how students would show the starting and ending points for the bookshelf measurement. Allow them to practice on several items in the room.
9. Summarize the lesson by reading *Math Counts: Length*. Have the students answer the questions presented in the book.

Assessment

- Give every student a piece of ribbon with a length several times shorter than the desk. Have them measure their desks using the ribbons. They should round their leftover amounts to the nearest whole number.

Notes to Teacher

- This lesson begins with a *Thinking About the Problem* section to encourage the students to think carefully about the process of solving a problem. Read the short scenario and allow the students to think about how they might solve the problem. Create a "Need to Know" board to use as a metacognitive planner and complete it with the students' responses to the following questions:
  - o What do we know?
  - o What do we need to know?
  - o How can we find out?

  Revisit the board at the end of the lesson to see whether they were able to solve the problem.
- You might consider allowing the students to go outside to demonstrate how big they think a pool should be as they ponder the *Thinking About the Problem* activity. In addition, the swimming pool measurement activities can easily be conducted on a field or sidewalk.

Extensions

The following student activities can be used to extend the lesson.

- Use the data from the footstep chart to have a discussion about median and mode.
- Prior to class, fold a piece of green cardstock into half so you end up with an 8.5" x 5.5" rectangle. Cut along the folded edge in a wavy motion to create two sets of "bushes." The bushes should be approximately 5" tall. Staple or tape the sheets together to make a strip of bushes with a final length of 72" (a little longer than the perimeter of the foam core board). Let the students decorate the bushes with branches, birds, and so forth. You will eventually attach the strips of bushes to the pool deck area to hide the bottom of the plastic container.

Lesson 8: Linear Measurement: Measuring Distance Using Nonstandard Units

Instructional Purpose

- To measure distance accurately using nonstandard units

Main Ideas

- Accurate measurements require identical units, precise starting and ending points, no gaps or overlaps in coverage, and partitioning of leftover (non-whole) units (measurement accuracy).
- The length of a larger unit may be made up of repeating smaller units (unit iteration).
- Sets of items may look different, but represent the same amount (equivalence).

Objectives

The students will be able to:

- Use representational units, such as walking strides or swimming strokes, to measure distance.
- Describe a situation where the starting point in a measurement is at the center.
- Characterize "leftover" units using mathematical terminology, such as "one half," "one third," and "one fourth."

Materials and Handouts

- Adding machine paper roll
- Blue painter's tape or masking tape
- Crayons
- Flat toothpicks
- Inner Tube Activity (Handout 8A)
- Beach Towel Activity (Handout 8B)
- Ribbon (cut into 12" lengths)
- Scissors
- Pool Diagram (Teacher Resource 8)
- 2" x 2" sticky notes cut in half to represent beach towels (three per student)
- 15" x 20" x 3/16" piece of foam core board (one piece per student)

Vocabulary

- Fraction
- Fourth
- Half
- Third

DOI: 10.4324/9781003238171-14

Activities

1. *Thinking About the Problem*: Read and discuss the following situation using the metacognitive planner discussed in the Notes to Teacher section. *The pool is done! Now it's time to have some fun. What are some of the ways we can measure distances in a pool?*
2. Introduce the lesson by taping a starting line on the floor. Have each student start with his or her foot behind the line. Ask each student to take a normal step. Using rolled adding machine paper, cut a strip the length of each student's stride. Have them compare their stride lengths to their cutout footprints by estimating how many footprints equal one stride. Verify by measuring. Discuss whether they could use strides to measure distance. Ask:
   - Could you use strokes to measure how far it is across a swimming pool?
   - Would everyone's stroke lengths be the same?

3. Remind the students about how they characterized "leftover" units in the previous lesson (e.g., "almost," "a little more than"). Talk about whether there is a more precise way they could characterize these leftover units. Remind them of the partitioning activity they did earlier where they divided the paper into equal segments. Introduce the ideas of "one half," "one third," and "one fourth."
4. Have students work in pairs. Distribute the **Inner Tube Activity (Handout 8A)** and have one student color and the other student cut it out (along the outside edge only; students should not cut out the middle). Students should write their names in the middle.
5. Using blue painter's tape or masking tape, lay out a large swimming pool model (approximately 8 ft x 10 ft) on the floor and have the students place their inner tubes anywhere in the pool. The teacher's inner tube should go exactly in the center of the **Pool Diagram (Teacher Resource 8)**. Talk about the distances between various inner tubes.
6. Give each pair of students a piece of ribbon approximately 12 inches long. Ask them to predict how many ribbon lengths their inner tube is from the teacher's inner tube, and then have them measure the actual distance. Point out that they should measure from the black dot in the center of each inner tube. Reiterate the importance of not leaving gaps or overlaps. Students should write their measurements on a chart (e.g., on the blackboard). The chart should have three columns: student pair names, predicted number of ribbon lengths, and measured distance. Talk about the similarities and differences in distances. Are some measurements whole numbers and others fractions?
7. Next, tell the students that you want each of them to be exactly the same distance away from your inner tube so that you can play a game. Discuss the strategies the students might use to figure out where to put their inner tubes. Once the students agree on a strategy (such as each of them measuring three ribbon lengths from the teacher's inner tube), have them actually move the inner tubes to the designated places. Ask:
   - What shape do the students' inner tubes make around the teacher's (circle)? Why?

Assessment

- Give each student the **Beach Towel Activity (Handout 8B)** and a flat toothpick. Using the toothpick as a measuring device, ask the students to draw two bottles of suntan lotion that are exactly the same distance away from the center of the beach towel.

Notes to Teacher

- This lesson begins with a *Thinking About the Problem* activity to encourage the students to think carefully about the process of solving a problem. Read the short scenario and allow the students to think about how they might solve the problem. Create a "Need to Know" board to use as a metacognitive planner and complete it with the students' responses to the following questions:
  - What do we know?
  - What do we need to know?
  - How can we find out?

  Revisit the board at the end of the lesson to see whether they were able to solve the problem.
- Young students sometimes have difficulty using their finger to mark the end of a measurement. To help them accurately compare their footsteps with their strides, have them make a pencil mark on the adding machine paper at the toe of their first footprint so they can exactly align the heel of their second footprint.
- Do not refer to the ribbons by their inch measurement yet. Once the students learn about standard units, you can refer back to the ribbons and talk about their actual lengths. This will help students to better visualize what 12" looks like.

Extension

The following student activities can be used to extend the lesson.

- Students may be curious about how to quantify "leftover" units when they don't fall exactly on a whole number or on one fourth, one third, or one half. Discuss the idea that there are many more fractions than the ones they discussed. Walk the students through folding an index card into eighths and describe the various fractions. Is there another way to talk about four eighths? How about six eighths?
- After students move their inner tubes to create a circle, have them move their inner tubes to create a square around the teacher's tube. Measure the various distances between their inner tubes and the teacher's and see what conclusions they can draw. This can lead to a discussion about diagonals and triangles.
- Distribute foam core boards and tell the students that this will represent the pool deck of their final project. Inform them that you will be cutting a hole in it for the pool later. Rather than assessing the students using the **Beach Towel Activity (Handout 8B)**, provide them with three cutouts of beach towels made from 2" x 2" sticky notes cut in half. (Make sure each half has a sticky section.) Using the toothpick as a measuring device, ask the students to place them on their foam core boards exactly the same distance apart. Students will measure the perimeter of these towels and glue them to the board during a later lesson.

Name: ______________________________ Date: ______________

Inner Tube Activity (Handout 8A)

Directions: Work with your partner. One student should color the inner tube. The other student should cut it out (along the outside edge only; **do not cut out the middle!**). Write your names in the middle. Follow your teacher's directions.

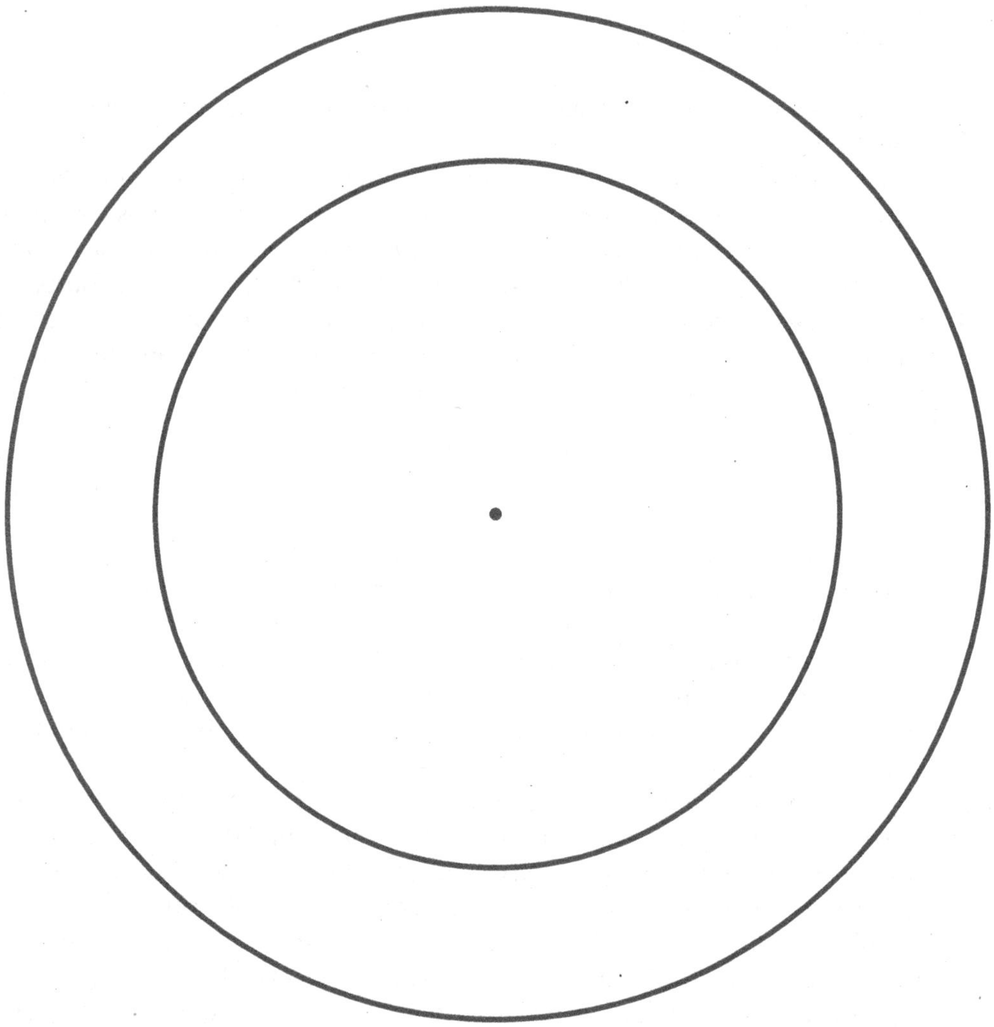

Name: ______________________ Date: ______________

Beach Towel Activity (Handout 8B)

Directions: Using the toothpick that your teacher gave you as a measuring device, draw two bottles of suntan lotion that are exactly the same distance away from the center of the beach towel.

Pool Diagram (Teacher Resource 8)

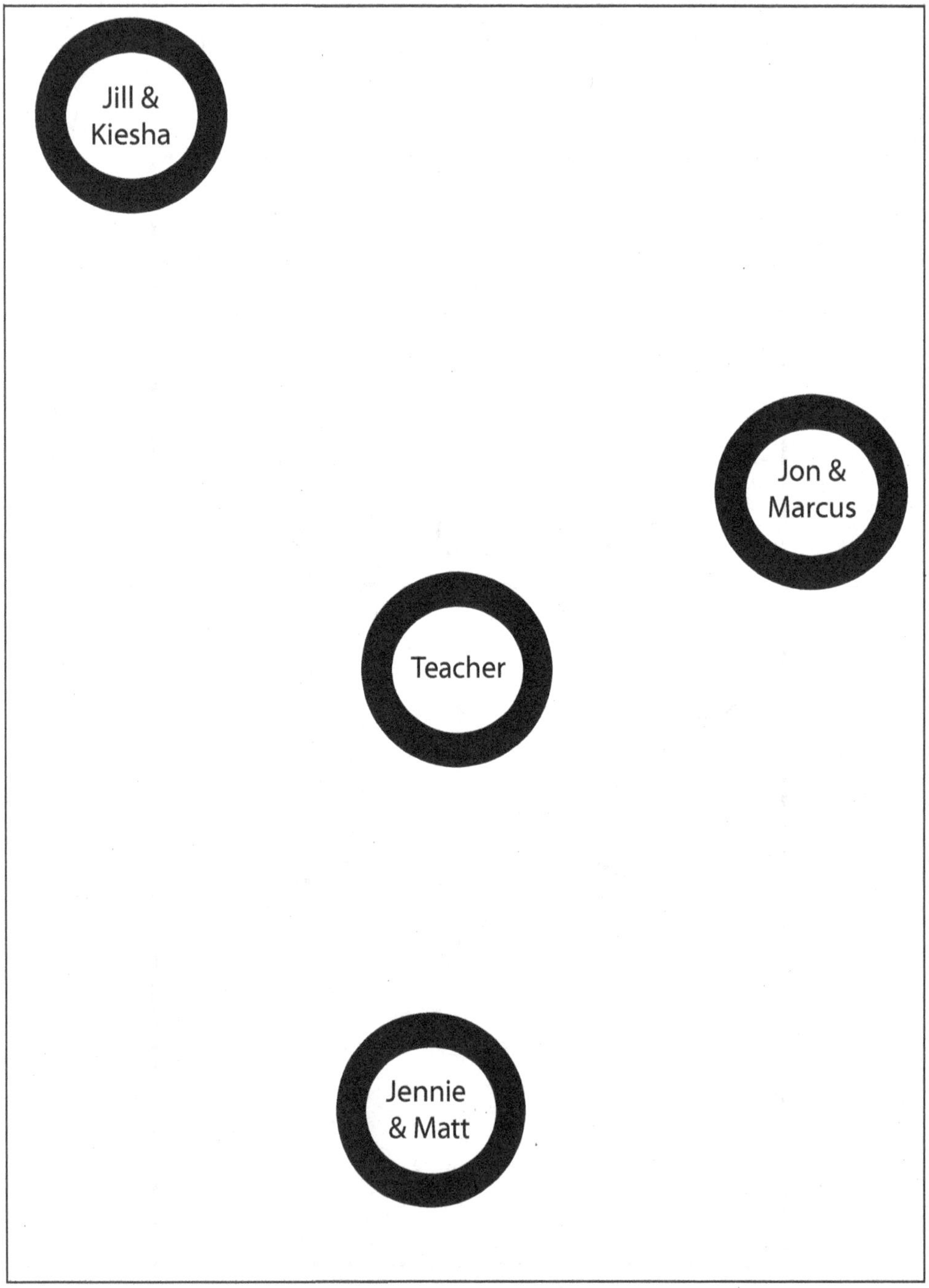

Lesson 9: Linear Measurement: Measuring Height Using Nonstandard Units

Instructional Purpose

- To measure height accurately using nonstandard units

Main Ideas

- The length of an object can be divided into equal-sized units (partitioning).
- The length of a larger unit may be made up of repeating smaller units (unit iteration).
- Knowing the relationship between one item and a second item, and the second item and a third item, one may deduce the relationship between the first item and third item (transitivity).
- Certain units convey what is being measured better than others (appropriate units).

Objectives

The students will be able to:

- Use an object shorter than the items to be measured to compare their heights using direct and indirect comparison.
- Use an object longer than the items to be measured to compare their heights using direct and indirect comparison.
- Explain why some nonstandard units make sense to measure height but others do not.

Materials and Handouts

- Books of various sizes
- Cardstock strip
- Counters
- Legos®
- Photos or pictures of a pool
- 6" dowels
- 12" dowels
- 8" tall box
- 10" tall box

Activities

1. *Thinking About the Problem*: Read and discuss the following situation using the metacognitive planner discussed in the Notes to Teacher section. *Many things at swimming pools can be measured using length, width, and depth, but there are some very important items that must be measured with the dimension of height. Can you think what they might be?* Show the students a photo or picture of a pool to help them identify items that would have a height measurement (e.g.,

DOI: 10.4324/9781003238171-15

the height of the fence surrounding a pool, the height of the rack holding buoys). Review how students measured length and distance over the previous days. Ask:

- How might measuring height be different?
- Could you use the same strategies?
- Could you use the same tools?
- Could you measure height with paces, like you measured the length of the swimming pool?

Discuss the similarities and differences between measuring length, distance, and height.

2. Provide each pair of students with a box (approximately 8" tall) to measure. Give them a 12" dowel and let them discover a way to measure the box. Discuss the different strategies they used. Remind them that not only can they partition the item being measured, but they can also partition the measurement tool. Discuss ideas about how they could partition the dowel to divide it into consistent units.
3. Give the students a box (approximately 10" tall) and ask them to measure the height using the same dowel. Discuss the comparisons they can make about the two boxes without directly comparing them.
4. Next, have the students measure the boxes using the 6" dowel. Discuss what they did when the dowel was too short to measure the entire height. Ask:
   - How do the measurements made with the short dowel compare with those made with the long dowel?

5. Divide the class into groups. At one table have a stack of various-sized books. At a separate table, have additional books put in various places. The books need to be of different thicknesses. Ask students to use the scattered books and build a stack that is the same height as the original stack. Tell them that they may only use one of the dowels to figure out how high they need to build the second stack; they may not make a direct comparison by moving the stacks together. Discuss the various strategies they used.
6. Next, scatter the second stack of books again. Give the students toothpicks and ask them to again make a second stack of books the same height as the first stack, using only the toothpicks to measure. Discuss which method was easier.
7. Remind the students about how they discussed scale models at the beginning of the unit. Ask them why people would want to build models that are smaller than real size. Show the students a simple tall structure made from Legos®. Design it with dimensions that can be evenly divided into halves, thirds, and fourths. Tell the students that you want them to make different-sized scale models of this structure. In groups, ask the students to build models that are one half, one third, and one fourth the height of the large structure. Discuss their strategies.

Assessment

- Give each student a stack of three Legos® and 20 counters. Tell the students they need to make the stack of counters three times as tall as the Legos® stack. Provide them with a cardstock strip to help them with their measurement.

Notes to Teacher

- This lesson begins with a *Thinking About the Problem* activity to encourage the students to think carefully about the process of solving a problem. Read the short scenario and allow the students to think about how they might solve the problem. Create a "Need to Know" board to use as a metacognitive planner and complete it with the students' responses to the following questions:
    - What do we know?
    - What do we need to know?
    - How can we find out?

- Revisit the board at the end of the lesson to see whether they were able to solve the problem.
- Do not refer to the dowels by their inch measurement yet. Simply referring to them as "the long dowel" and "the short dowel" will suffice. Once the students learn about standard units, you can refer back to the dowels and talk about their actual lengths. This will help students to better visualize what 6" and 12" look like.

Extension

The following student activity can be used to extend the lesson.

- Allow the students to measure the height of various items in the classroom using one of the dowels. Record the heights on the board. Have the students create a line plot of how many items are one dowel length, two dowel lengths, and so forth.

Lesson 10: Linear Measurement: Measuring Length Using Standard Units

Instructional Purpose

- To introduce standard units
- To measure accurately using standard measurement tools

Main Ideas

- Accurate measurements require identical units, precise starting and ending points, no gaps or overlaps in coverage, and partitioning of leftover (non-whole) units (measurement accuracy).
- Using what you know about an object may be helpful in making an educated guess about the numerical approximation of an object (estimation).

Objectives

The students will be able to:

- Explain why standard units are needed for measurement.
- Show where measurement should begin on a ruler (ignoring the leading edge).
- Estimate the length of an object given another object of similar length.

Materials

- Blocks of various sizes
- Crayons or markers
- *Millions to Measure* by David Schwartz (HarperCollins)
- Precut outlines (e.g., of yourself, of your principal) on large paper roll
- Rulers with inches and centimeters
- Drink umbrellas to represent table umbrellas
- Foam swimming pool noodle (cut into 3/4" slices) to form tabletop
- Hot glue
- Paper party nut containers for base of table (small paper cups such as those used for ketchup at fast-food restaurants)
- Students' plastic "pools"
- 3" x 3" adhesive shipping labels

Vocabulary

- Centimeters
- Estimate
- Inches
- Metric units
- Ruler
- U.S. customary units

DOI: 10.4324/9781003238171-16

Activities

1. *Thinking About the Problem*: Read and discuss the following situation using the metacognitive planner discussed in the Notes to Teacher section. *When the construction workers built the swimming pool, they wanted to make sure they made it the same length as the other swimming pools around town. Why would they want to do this?*
2. Show the students a stack of five small blocks. Talk about how tall the stack is, relating the number of blocks to the number of units ("five blocks high"). Use a different-sized block to create another stack that is five blocks high. Ask:
   - Why isn't "five blocks high" the same height in both cases?
   - If someone said that something was "five blocks high," how might that cause confusion?
   - How could this kind of confusion be fixed?

   Lead students' responses into a discussion of standard units.
3. Distribute rulers and ask the students if they notice anything about the ends of their rulers. Point out the fact that the units don't actually start at the end of the ruler. (Most rulers have a leading edge.) Talk about how some rulers have different types of units (inches and centimeters). Explain that we commonly use U.S. customary units in the United States (e.g., inches, feet, yards), but scientists and many people in other parts of the world use metric units (e.g., millimeters, centimeters, meters). Model how to measure something so that students understand how to line the ruler up.
4. Draw models of several items on the board and remind the students how to draw an arrow from their starting point to their ending point. Demonstrate how they would measure each item using inches. Give the students an opportunity to measure various items in the classroom.
5. Once the students are comfortable using a ruler, have them measure one object and estimate the size of another object. Ask them to verify their estimations by measuring the second object. To practice estimation, have each student work with a partner. Have one partner estimate the size of an object while the other partner measures it to verify. After students do this, they should switch roles.
6. Discuss the various "measuring tools" (e.g., ribbons, dowels) the students have previously used and ask them to predict the length of them. Have them measure the items to verify their predictions.
7. Read the book *Millions to Measure* and discuss the history of measurement. Ask:
   - How does this impact how we measure today?

   Relate this to the assessment activity where students will be measuring various body parts.

Assessment

- Create several life-sized models (outlines) of yourself or the principal (lying down on the floor) ahead of time. Tell the students that you want to know how far out you can walk in the pool before your head is entirely under water. Begin the activity by measuring an item close to your height (such as a supply cabinet) and telling the students how tall it is. Ask them to estimate your height based on this. Divide the students into groups and give each group an outline. Have them measure your height on the outline and write it at the top of the paper. Ask the students to measure various parts of the outline—your arm, leg, torso, and so forth. They should write each measurement down, drawing an arrow from their starting point to their ending point. When they are done measuring, ask them to draw a bathing suit on the outline as if you were going to the pool. Hang the outlines around the classroom. If there is ample time, allow the students to make outlines of each other to measure and decorate.

Notes to Teacher

- This lesson begins with a *Thinking About the Problem* activity to encourage the students to think carefully about the process of solving a problem. Read the short scenario and allow the students to think about how they might solve the problem. Create a "Need to Know" board to use as a metacognitive planner and complete it with the students' responses to the following questions:
  - What do we know?
  - What do we need to know?
  - How can we find out?

  Revisit the board at the end of the lesson to see whether students were able to solve the problem.
- As students gain confidence with measurement using inches, try the same activities using centimeters.

Extension

The following student activities can be used to extend the lesson.

- Have each student work with a partner. Have one student choose a measurement amount (such as 5 inches). The student's partner must draw a line or a shape of that length. The first student must verify the drawing by measuring it also. Reverse roles.
- Type or write the following on a 3" x 3" adhesive label for each student:
  - Length of pool:
  - Width of pool:
  - Depth of deep end:
  - Depth of shallow end:
  - Width of pool lanes:
  - Perimeter of pool:

  On another 3" x 3" adhesive label, type or write the following:
  - Height of umbrella:
  - Height of table:
  - Height of fence posts:
  - Perimeter of deck:
  - Perimeter of beach towel:

- Have the students measure the length and width of the plastic container as well as the depth of the shallow and deep ends of the pool. They should record their measurements on the appropriate adhesive label. Keep the adhesive backing on the labels; the students will stick them onto the foam core at a later time.
- Prior to class, pre-cut foam swimming pool "noodles" into slices, approximately 3/4" thick. Hot glue the foam on top of a 1" paper party nut container to create a table. Have the students measure the table and record its height on their labels. Next, have them measure the height of an unopened party drink umbrella and

record the measurement on their labels. Poke the umbrella through the hole in the foam noodle and into the nut container. To make the umbrella stand up straight, poke the bottom of it into another piece of foam noodle hidden under the nut container. Do not allow the students to open their umbrellas until the project is complete.

Lesson 11: Linear Measurement: Appropriate Units and Tools

Instructional Purpose

- To familiarize students with various measurement tools and their uses

Main Ideas

- The larger the unit, the smaller the number of units needed to measure a particular object; the smaller the unit, the larger the number of units needed to measure that same object (inverse relationship between size of units and number of units).
- Certain units convey what is being measured better than others (appropriate units).
- Certain tools work better than others to measure the same attributes (appropriate tools).

Objectives

The students will be able to:

- Identify various tools to measure length.
- Select appropriate units to measure various items.
- Choose an appropriate tool to measure various items.

Materials and Handouts

- Blue painter's tape or masking tape
- Hardware tape measure
- Meterstick
- Ruler
- Sewing tape measure
- Sticky notes
- Trundle wheel
- Yardstick
- Yarn
- tape
- Students' plastic "pools"
- Students' 3" x 3" adhesive labels (do not remove backing)
- Yarn cut into lengths 2" longer than the length of the plastic container

Vocabulary

- Meterstick
- Tape measure
- Trundle wheel
- Yardstick

DOI: 10.4324/9781003238171-17

Activities

1. *Thinking About the Problem*: Read and discuss the following situation using the metacognitive planner discussed in the Notes to Teacher section. *The builders forgot to label how deep the pool is at the shallow and deep ends. What tool should they use to measure the depth, and how should they talk about the units?*
2. Introduce the lesson by talking about the various measuring tools the students have seen their parents use at home. Ask:
    - What do all of them have in common?
    - How are they different?

3. Show the students a yardstick, talk about its properties, and show students how to read it. Compare a ruler to a yardstick. Show students tape measures, both the hardware type and the sewing type, and demonstrate how to read them. Talk about the units. Show students a meterstick and talk about its units.
4. Talk about the different tools different people use in their jobs. Ask:
    - What kind of measuring tools might a builder use?
    - What would someone who sews clothes use?
    - What tool do parents use to measure their child's height?
    - What tool could they use to measure their waist?
    - Why doesn't everyone use the same tool for measuring?

5. Have a variety of measurement tools available for the students. Allow them to choose one and ask them to measure the length of the room. (They can do this individually or in groups.) Write down their measurements and discuss. Talk about which tool was easiest to handle. Ask:
    - Does it make more sense to talk about the length of a room in terms of inches or feet?
    - If students were measuring the length of a swimming pool, what unit would they use?
    - What tool would they use to measure the swimming pool's length?
    - If students were talking about distance in a car, what unit would they use?

    Remind students that the larger the unit, the smaller the number of units needed to measure a particular object.
6. Using the trundle wheel, have a student measure 2 meters. Have another student measure 2 meters with the meterstick. Ask:
    - Are the measurements the same?

7. Tape a piece of yarn around the trundle wheel and unroll it onto the ground as the trundle wheel moves around so that the students can understand that even though the measuring device looks round, it is still making a linear measurement. Ask:
    - Are there any other measurement tools that measure the same length?

8. Distribute small sticky notes for the students to measure. Have them select a different measurement tool than they used previously to measure the room. Again, talk about which tool was the easiest to use. Ask:
    - What unit makes the most sense in this situation?

Assessment

- Using blue tape or masking tape, tape models of several medium-sized "baby pools" on the ground and ask the students to measure the length of them using a measurement tool of their choosing. Ask them to explain the units they used and why they selected a specific tool.

Notes to Teacher

- This lesson begins with a *Thinking About the Problem* section to encourage the students to think carefully about the process of solving a problem. Read the short scenario and allow the students to think about how they might solve the problem. Create a "Need to Know" board to use as a metacognitive planner and complete it with the students' responses to the following questions:
    - What do we know?
    - What do we need to know?
    - How can we find out?

  Revisit the board at the end of the lesson to see whether they were able to solve the problem.

Extension

The following student activities can be used to extend the lesson.

- Have the students measure the swimming pool in centimeters, inches, feet, yards, and meters. Make a chart of equivalent measurements.
- Using the students' length measurement of the plastic container, cut five pieces of yarn approximately 2 inches longer than the length to create the lane lines for the pool. Help the students tape the yarn onto the lane line locations they previously marked on their containers. The extra inch of yarn on each end should be taped under the edge of the plastic container. Ask them to measure the width of a single pool lane using an appropriate tool and record the measurement on the adhesive labels.

Lesson 12: Measuring Perimeter

Instructional Purpose

- To introduce the concept of perimeter

Main Ideas

- Objects with different attributes are measured in different ways (appropriate measurement).
- An item remains the same length even when placed in a different position (conservation).
- Certain units convey what is being measured better than others (appropriate units).
- Certain tools work better than others to measure different-sized objects or distances.
- Using what you know about an object may be helpful in making an educated guess about the numerical approximation of an object (estimation).

Objectives

The students will be able to:

- Explain why one would want to determine the perimeter of an object.
- Estimate the perimeter of an object.
- Find the perimeter of regularly shaped objects.
- Select appropriate units for measurement.

Materials and Handouts

- Blue painter's tape or masking tape
- Crayons
- Decorated 4"x 6" index card (representing a beach towel)
- Glue
- Tile Activity (Handout 12A)
- Star Activity (Handout 12B)
- Ribbon or rick-rack trim (30" per person)
- Rulers
- Scissors
- Tape measure
- Two "baby pools" from Lesson 11, one cut slightly smaller than the other
- 5"x 8" unlined index cards
- ≈ Assembled student "pools" including deck
- ≈ Awl or other device for poking fencepost holes in the foam core board
- ≈ Clear packing tape or hot glue
- ≈ Students' 1" x 2" "beach towels"
- ≈ 12" pipe cleaners (10 per student)

Vocabulary

- Approximate
- Perimeter

DOI: 10.4324/9781003238171-18

Activities

1. *Thinking About the Problem*: Read and discuss the following situation using the metacognitive planner discussed in the Notes to Teacher section. *The builders have decided that they want to put a fence around the swimming pool and locker rooms. How should they determine how long to make the fence?*
2. Explain that the term "perimeter" refers to the measurement around the outside edge of an object. Demonstrate how one would measure the perimeter of several objects in the classroom. Ask the students to talk about a swimming pool and different things they could find the perimeter of there (the pool edge, surface of the diving board, kickboard, tiles, and so on).
3. Discuss the reasons why one would want to find a perimeter (e.g., to determine the length of the wood for building a sandbox, how much ribbon to wrap around a present, a fence for their pet). Ask:
   - Could somebody use a scale model to figure out the perimeter of something?
4. Have the students find the perimeter of the classroom by pacing. Ask:
   - Is this an exact measurement or an approximate measurement?
5. Have the students actually measure the perimeter. Discuss the similarities and differences between the measurements.
6. Using blue painter's tape or masking tape, tape a large and a small "baby pool" model on the ground and have the students measure its perimeter. Talk about the tools and units they used. Ask:
   - Could they use any tool to measure the pool?
   - Would it make sense to use any tool?
7. Write the perimeter measurement on the board. Now tape a slightly smaller baby pool model and ask students to estimate its perimeter based on the perimeter of the larger pool. Have them check their estimate by measuring.
8. Give each student the **Tile Activity (Handout 12A)** and ask them to determine the perimeter of Tile 1. Talk about the strategies they used for measuring the tile. Have the students estimate the perimeter of Tile 2. (It's the same as the perimeter of Tile 1.) Ask:
   - Why do students think it has the same or a different perimeter?
9. Have students measure Tile 2 and discuss their findings. Ask them to estimate the perimeter of Tile 3. Ask:
   - Is it larger or smaller than Tile 1?
   - Why?
10. Have the students measure Tile 3. If time permits, encourage the students to decorate and cut out their tiles and hang them around the classroom.
11. Give the students the **Star Activity (Handout 12B)** and allow them to use any tool of their choosing to determine the perimeter of the star. Have them discuss their reasoning for the tools and strategies they used for measuring the star. Ask:
    - Did students discover any shortcuts?

Assessment

- Hand the students a 5" x 8" index card and tell them it is a model of a beach towel. Explain that they are going to decorate it by putting trim all the way around the edges of it. They need to find the perimeter of the paper so that they can cut the exact length of ribbon to glue onto their towel. Show them a completed 4" x 6" index card "towel" and explain that you found the perimeter of your towel to be 20". On one side of their index card, ask them to write down what they estimate the perimeter of their towel to be. Then hand them rulers and have them determine the actual perimeter. When they have finished gluing the ribbon around the edges, have them decorate their towels and hang them around the classroom.

Notes to Teacher

- This lesson begins with a *Thinking About the Problem* section to encourage the students to think carefully about the process of solving a problem. Read the short scenario and allow the students to think about how they might solve the problem. Create a "Need to Know" board to use as a metacognitive planner and complete it with the students' responses to the following questions:
  - o What do we know?
  - o What do we need to know?
  - o How can we find out?

  Revisit the board at the end of the lesson to see whether they were able to solve the problem.
- So that students can focus on the concept of perimeter rather than becoming distracted with fractions, make sure that the measurements of the sides of the objects the students initially measure have whole-number measurements.

Extension

The following student activities can be used to extend the lesson.

- Have the students measure items that do not have whole-number measurements for their sides so they can practice adding fractions.
- Ask the students to describe the shape of a fence they have seen. Ask:
  - o Are all fences rectangular?
  - o What other shapes can fences come in?
  - o Could a fence be in a circle?
- Draw an irregularly shaped fence on the board. How would students go about determining the perimeter? Discuss the various strategies they might use. Have the students find the perimeter of irregular shapes.
- Partner the students. Have one student choose a perimeter amount (such as 36"). The student's partner must draw a shape with a perimeter of that amount. The first student must verify the drawing by measuring it. Once students have done this, they should reverse roles.
- Prior to class, poke a hole near the edge of each corner of the foam core board with an awl. Poke another hole in the middle of each side of the board so that you end up with eight holes. Cut a hole in the middle the foam core board large enough so that the plastic container can drop down into it. The lip of the plastic container should overlap the foam core board. Using hot glue or clear packing tape, affix the container to the foam core board.

- Have the students measure the perimeters of the pool and the pool deck. They should write their measurements on their labels.
- Give the students their 1" x 2" "beach towels" from the earlier lesson and have them measure the perimeter and write their measurements on their label. Glue the towels to the pool deck, making sure to leave room at two corners of the pool deck for the labels.
- Talk about how the students can use the pool deck perimeter to figure out how long to make their fence. Pre-cut pipe cleaner into eight 4" pieces to form vertical fence posts. Have the students install the fence posts by poking the pipe cleaner into the hole and bending it underneath the board to hold it into place. Twist seven 12" pieces of pipe cleaner together to make to make the horizontal portion of the fence and attach it to the vertical posts by bending the top of the vertical pipe cleaner over the horizontal strand of pipe cleaner. Help the students twist together the two ends of the horizontal pipe cleaners to make an enclosed area. Have them measure the height of their fence posts and record it on their label.

Name: ______________________________ Date: ______________

Tile Activity (Handout 12A)

Directions: Figure out the perimeter of Tile 1.

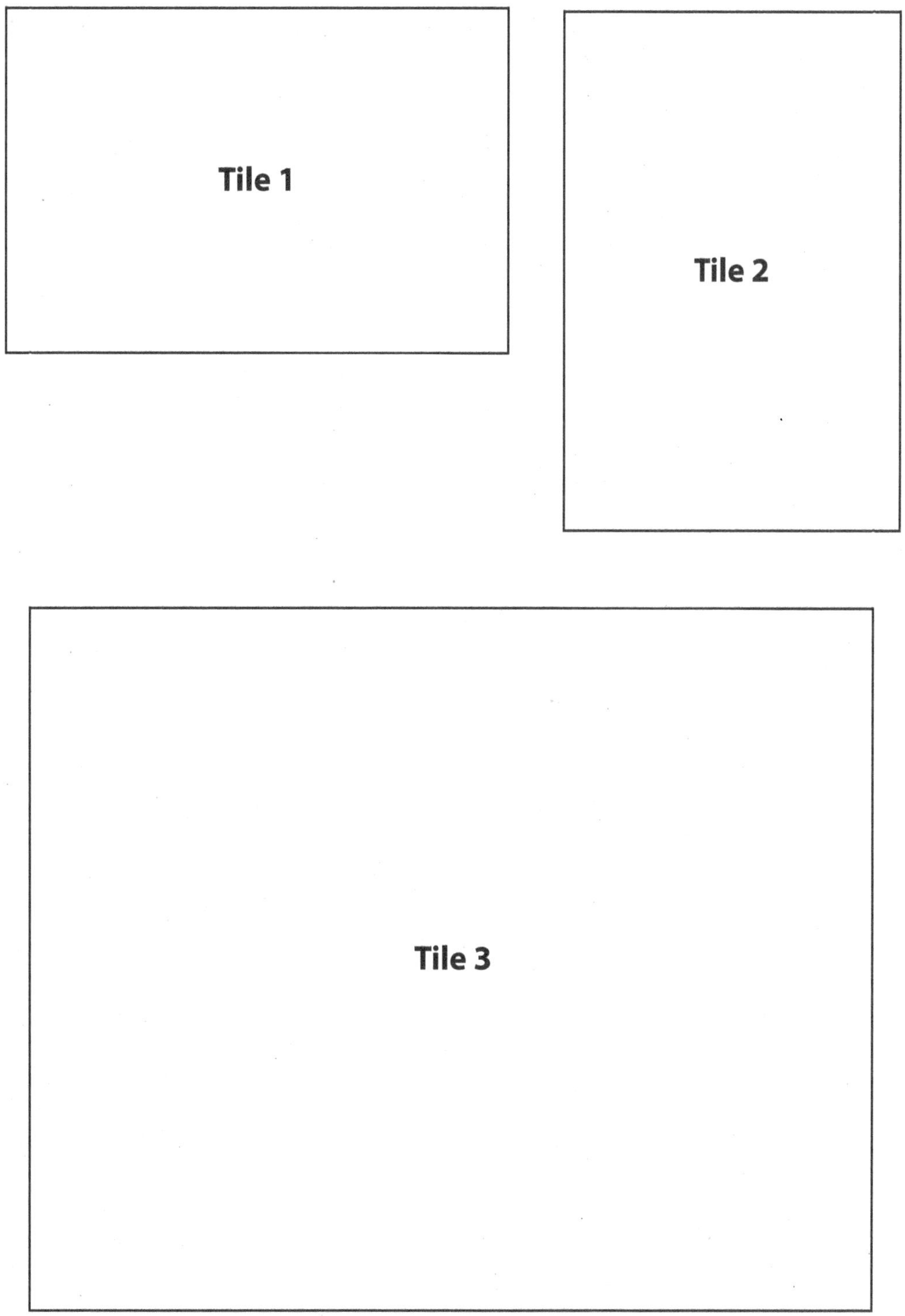

Name: ______________________________ Date: ______________

Star Activity (Handout 12B)

Directions: Use any tool of your choice to figure out the perimeter of the star.

Lesson 13: Postassessment

Instructional Purpose

- To assess student knowledge and understanding of unit topics

Main Idea

- Objects with different attributes are measured in different ways (appropriate measurement).

Objective

The student will be able to:

- Demonstrate an understanding of models, problem solving, and measurement concepts.

Materials and Handouts

- Container with various-sized objects (one for each table)
- Same Height Activity (Handout 13A)
- Three Times as Tall Activity (Handout 13B)
- One Third as Tall Activity (Handout 13C)
- Lego® piece (2")
- Paper

Activities

1. The unit postassessment is broken into three parts: math content, math processes, and overarching concept. Begin the assessment with the math content activity. When students are finished, divide the class into two groups. One group will meet with you to complete the math process assessment, while the others will work on their own to complete the overarching concept assessment. Then switch groups.
2. *Math content* (representation, measuring, estimation, comparing): Place a container with many classroom objects of various sizes at each table. Hold up a Lego® piece and tell the students it is 2" tall. Ask them to look in the container to find an object that is the same height as the Lego®. When they find an object, they should trace its shape on the **Same Height Activity (Handout 13A)** and then return the object to the box. Allow 5 minutes for this activity. Next, ask students to find something that is about three times as tall as the Lego® piece and to trace its shape on the **Three Times as Tall Activity (Handout 13B)**. Allow 5 minutes for this activity. Repeat the activity a final time, this time asking students to find items that are a third as tall as the Lego® piece and to trace these items on the **One Third as Tall Activity (Handout 13C)**. (Scoring guide: 1 point for each item that is about the same size as the Lego® piece; 1 point for each item that is about three times as tall, and 1 point for each item that is one third as tall).
3. *Math processes* (problem solving): Tell the students that you want to build a doghouse for your dog. Ask them to answer the following question: "If you wanted to build a doghouse in your backyard, what would you have to know before you built it?" Take notes of their responses or ask students to record their

DOI: 10.4324/9781003238171-19

individual responses on paper, into a tape recorder, or through use of a scribe (e.g., volunteer, aide, older student). (Scoring guide: 1 point for each different reasonable response.)

4. *Overarching concept* (models): Ask the students to draw a model of the school's playground, making it as accurate as possible. (Scoring guide: 1 point for each correct item; 1 point for each item that is in the correct location.)

Notes to Teacher

- Select items for the container that are easy for the students to trace so that you can quickly identify what the objects are.

Extension

The following student activities can be used to extend the lesson.

- To complete the pool, attach the strip of bushes the students decorated previously to the edge of the foam core board to hide the plastic container and the bottoms of the fence posts from view. The bushes hang better if you crease them at the pool deck corners.
- Affix the students' measurement labels to a corner of the swimming pool deck.
- Return the students' tables and umbrellas and have them place them on the pool deck.

Name: ____ Date: ____________________

Same Height Activity (Handout 13A)

Directions: Trace an item from the container that is the same height as the Lego® piece.

Name: ______________________________ Date: ______________

Three Times as Tall Activity (Handout 13B)

Directions: Trace an item from the container that is three times as tall as the Lego® piece.

Name: ____ Date: ____________________

One Third as Tall Activity (Handout 13C)

Directions: Trace an item from the container that is one third as tall as the Lego® piece.

Part Three: Unit Extension and Resources

Unit Extension: Building a Pool Activity

Overview

The students will create a model swimming pool using a plastic container and foam core board. The finished pool will include a pool bottom, lane lines, a pool deck, a fence, bushes, beach towels, and a patio table with an umbrella. The students will measure perimeter, length, width, height, and depth dimensions and record their measurements on labels. The following description depicts the *Building a Pool* activity as a whole; however, this activity may be broken into any number of segments and completed as part of a math lesson or during center time. If you decide to divide this activity into shorter segments, *Building a Pool* extension activities are suggested in several of the lesson plans and are identified with a wave symbol.

Materials

- Awl or other device for poking fence post holes in the foam core board
- Clear packing tape
- Clear tape
- Drink umbrellas to represent table umbrellas
- Foam swimming pool noodle to form table tops (cut into segments)
- Hot glue
- Markers
- Paper party nut containers for base of tables
- Stapler
- Yarn for creating lane lines
- 2" x 2" sticky notes cut in half to represent towels (three per student)
- 3" x 3" adhesive shipping labels (two per student)
- 3" x 5" sticky notes (two per student)
- 6-quart plastic container with lid (outside dimensions approximately 13" length x 8" width x 4.5" depth; one per student)
- 8.5" x 11" green cardstock (five pages per student)
- 12" pipe cleaners (nine per student)
- 12" x 12" blue cardstock (one page per student)
- 15" x 20" x 3/16" piece of foam core board (one per student)

Activities

1. **Labels:** Type or write the following on a 3" x 3" adhesive label for each student:
   - Length of pool:
   - Width of pool:
   - Depth of deep end:
   - Depth of shallow end:
   - Width of pool lanes:
   - Perimeter of pool:

   On another 3" x 3" adhesive label, type or write the following:
   - Height of umbrella:
   - Height of table:
   - Height of fence posts:

DOI: 10.4324/9781003238171-21

- Perimeter of deck:
- Perimeter of beach towel:

As the students create the elements of the project, have them write their measurements on the labels. You may wish to store the labels inside each student's plastic container so they can easily find them to record additional measurements. At the completion of the project, affix each label to a corner of the swimming pool deck.

2. **Pool:** Pre-cut a piece of blue cardstock that will fit lengthwise inside the plastic container angling from the bottom of the container (deep end) to about the middle of the container's height (shallow end). This represents the bottom of the pool. For a more realistic pool, cut the plastic container lid into the same shape and hot glue it to the container so that the students can actually fill the pool with water. Have the students measure the length and width of the pool as well as the depth of the pool at the shallow and deep ends. They should also determine the perimeter of the pool.
3. **Lane lines:** Using the students' pool length measurements, cut five pieces of yarn approximately 2" longer than the length to create the lane lines for the pool. Provide the students with a piece of paper the width of the pool. Have them divide it into sixths to represent the six lanes of the pool. Have them record the width of a single lane on their labels. Help them to hold their paper against each end of the plastic container and mark the location of each fold (or line) to indicate where they will attach their lane lines. Help the students tape the yarn onto the lane line locations. The extra inch of yarn on each end should be taped under the edge of the plastic container.
4. **Beach towels:** Cut colorful 2" x 2" sticky notes in half to create 1" x 2" beach towels. Students may wish to decorate them. Have the students measure the perimeter of their beach towels and write their measurements on their labels. Glue the towels to the pool deck, making sure to leave room at two corners of the pool deck for the labels.
5. **Pool deck:** Have the students measure the perimeter of the pool deck and record it on their labels. Cut a hole in the middle of the foam core board large enough so that the plastic container can drop down into it. The lip of the plastic container should overlap the foam core board. Hot glue or tape the pool into place using clear packing tape.
6. **Fence:** Talk about how the students can use the pool deck perimeter to figure out how long to make their fence. Cut pipe cleaner into eight 4" pieces to form vertical fence posts. Poke a hole near the edge of each corner of the foam core board with an awl. Poke another hole in the middle of each side of the board so that you have eight holes. Have the students install the fence posts by poking the pipe cleaner up into the hole and bending it underneath the board to hold it into place. Twist six 12" pieces of pipe cleaner together to make to make the horizontal portion of the fence and attach it to the vertical posts by bending the tops of the vertical pipe cleaners over the horizontal strand of pipe cleaner. Help the students twist together the two ends of the horizontal pipe cleaners to make an enclosed area. Have students measure the height of their fence posts and record it on their label.
7. **Bushes:** Fold a piece of green cardstock in half so you have an 8.5" x 5.5" rectangle. Cut along the folded edge in a wavy motion to create two sets of "bushes." The bushes should end up to be approximately 5" tall. Staple or tape the sheets together to make a strip of bushes with a final length of 72" (a little longer than

the perimeter of the foam core board). Let the students decorate the bushes with branches, birds, and so forth. Attach the strip of bushes to the edge of the foam core board with hot glue to hide the plastic container and bottom of the fence posts from view. The bushes hang better if you crease them at the pool deck corners.

8. **Table and umbrella:** Have the students measure the height of a party drink umbrella and record the measurement on their labels. Cut foam swimming pool noodles into slices, approximately 3/4" thick. Hot glue a slice to the top of a 1" paper party nut container to create a table and have the students measure and record its total height. Poke the umbrella through the hole in the foam noodle and into the nut container. To make the umbrella stand up straight, poke the bottom of it into another piece of foam noodle hidden under the nut container.

References

Battista, M. (2006). Understanding the development of students' thinking about length. *Teaching Children Mathematics, 13*, 140–146.

Common Core State Standards Initiative. (2010). *The standards: Mathematics*. Retrieved from http://www.corestandards.org/assets/CCSSI_Math%20Standards.pdf

Hatfield, M. M., Edwards, N. T., Bitter, G. G., & Morrow, J. (2000). *Mathematics methods for elementary and middle school teachers* (4th ed.). New York, NY: John Wiley & Sons.

National Council of Teachers of Mathematics. (2010). *Principles and standards for school mathematics*. Reston, VA: Author.

Rogers, K. (2008, March). *An update on research in gifted education*. Paper presented at the 13th Annual National Curriculum Network Conference, The College of William and Mary, Center for Gifted Education, Williamsburg, VA.

Common Core State Standards

Lesson	Common Core State Standards in Math
Lesson 2: Models	K.G.B Analyze, compare, create, and compose shapes.
Lesson 3: Dimensions	K.MD.A Describe and compare measurable attributes.
	K.G.A Identify and describe shapes.
	K.G.B Analyze, compare, create, and compose shapes.
	1.G.A Reason with shapes and their attributes.
Lesson 4: Comparing and Ordering Objects	K.MD.A Describe and compare measurable attributes.
	1.MD.A Measure lengths indirectly and by iterating length units.
Lesson 5: Partitioning	K.CC.C Compare numbers.
	K.MD.A Describe and compare measurable attributes.
	1.G.A Reason with shapes and their attributes.
	2.G.A Reason with shapes and their attributes.
Lesson 6: Comparing Length by Rearranging Parts	K.MD.A Describe and compare measurable attributes.
	1.MD.A Measure lengths indirectly and by iterating length units.
Lesson 7: Measuring Length Using Nonstandard Units	K.MD.A Describe and compare measurable attributes.
	1.MD.A Measure lengths indirectly and by iterating length units.
Lesson 8: Measuring Distance Using Nonstandard Units	K.MD.A Describe and compare measurable attributes.
	1.MD.A Measure lengths indirectly and by iterating length units.
	1.G.A Reason with shapes and their attributes.
	2.G.A Reason with shapes and their attributes.
	3.NF.A Develop understanding of fractions as numbers.
Lesson 9: Measuring Height Using Nonstandard Units	K.MD.A Describe and compare measurable attributes.
	1.MD.A Measure lengths indirectly and by iterating length units.
Lesson 10: Measuring Length Using Standard Units	K.MD.A Describe and compare measurable attributes.
	1.MD.A Measure lengths indirectly and by iterating length units.
	2.MD.A Measure and estimate lengths in standard units.
Lesson 11: Appropriate Units and Tools	K.MD.A Describe and compare measurable attributes.
	1.MD.A Measure lengths indirectly and by iterating length units.
	2.MD.A Measure and estimate lengths in standard units.
Lesson 12: Measuring Perimeter	K.MD.A Describe and compare measurable attributes.
	2.MD.A Measure and estimate lengths in standard units.
	3.MD.D Geometric measurement: recognize perimeter.